VISION

From Invisible to Visible

Turn Your Vision into Reality

Dr. Claudette Morgan-Scott

ISBN 978-1-64191-637-0 (paperback)
ISBN 978-1-64191-639-4 (hardcover)
ISBN 978-1-64191-638-7 (digital)

Christian Faith Publishing, Inc.
832 Park Avenue
Meadville, PA 16335
www.christianfaithpublishing.com

Printed in the United States of America

Dedication

My two beautiful daughters, Lertisha and Sharna, you are my gift from God; you both have brought me so much joy. I have watched you gracefully make endless sacrifices growing up in the home of a Kingdom Leader. The Lord taught us how to navigate the difficult terrains together; which has made us closer, stronger and wiser. It has been a pleasure to see you become successful, God-fearing women, of great virtue, impacting and changing the world. Love you dearly my adorable princesses; you will forever walk in the favor of the Lord. Your virtue, what you carry cannot be compared to the wealth of this world. I speak blessings over you and great success in all that you endeavor to achieve; I am honored to be your mother.

Forward

Dr. Claudette Morgan-Scott has put together a volume that every leader will benefit from. Her personal transparency regarding her own struggles and the pains of leadership will touch you deeply. Her journey into wholeness and an anointing as a reformational leader will encourage and inspire you greatly. Her practical and applicable revelation of HOW a ministry can stay on the cutting edge, be fluid, develop leaders AND influence culture will motivate you to arise in your Calling like never before! You need this book!

Bob Long
Apostolic Founder/Director of Rally Call Ministries, Leadership Network and Institute

Acknowledgements

I am grateful, the Lord is truly my heartbeat, the reason I exist, why I have a purpose and hope. I feel the immense love that my heavenly Father has toward me; that even in times of successes and failures His love towards me has never wavered.

I honor my precious Mother, Pearl. You have been a wonderful example of a Godly woman, who extends yourself to meet the needs of others. You are truly a Pearl of great value.

During this process, the Lord has taken the Shiloh Worship Center Family on a journey. The Lord has tested our faith and confidence in the Him. He has allowed us to be sensitive to His voice, while resting in His ability to lead and guide us as we pioneered through new territory. I am so grateful for the Shiloh family, without you, this book would not have been possible. We had experienced great successes, laughed together, cried together, celebrated together, prayed together, but most of all endevoured to advance the Kingdom of God together; we are truly a family. You supported me while I grew in my Apostolic leadership and have taken this faith walk with me. We have gained wisdom, knowledge, and understanding shifting the invisible into the visible realm. Thank you for my dear Shiloh family; your future is great, God bless the works of your hands and may your generations be blessed.

The Lord has undergirded me with a great team of Kingdom-minded leaders. I thank them for what they have contributed to my development, growth, and most of all, for their support.

I acknowledge all leaders advancing the Kingdom of God. I salute you and pray for you daily. I celebrate your successes; in Christ, we win.

Contents

Forward...v

Acknowledgements...vii

Introduction...11

Part One
The Birth of a Vision..19

Chapter 1.   Subpoenaed by Heaven.............................21

Chapter 2.   Birthing the Vision: My Story..................56

Chapter 3.   Imparting the Vision 73

Chapter 4.   Vision Blockers...88

Part Two
A Guided Tour through Vision Development............................109

Chapter 5.   Purpose of Heart......................................111

Chapter 6.   The Brilliant Business Model 126

Chapter 7.   Spiritual Activism 148

Chapter 8.   A Working Model.....................................163

Chapter 9.   Strategies for Success...............................176

Chapter 10. Conclusion 186

Appendix 1. The 21/21 Model...193

Appendix 2. Vision Emergence Template (VET) 195

Bibliography..197

References 201

The Future 205

Introduction

Many have asked the question, what is my purpose in life? And, how do I fulfill my purpose? We must understand that God has a plan and a purpose for us, "Many are the plans in a person's heart, but it is the Lord's purpose that prevails" (Proverbs 19:21). The book of Exodus tells us that Moses, an Israelite, was born into a cultural group that was experiencing oppression while living in Egypt. The Israelites were in Egypt for four hundred and thirty years, most of that time as slaves (Exodus 12:40-41). Even though the Israelites were in bondage, the population was growing rapidly. As a form of population reduction the Egyptians ordered the midwives to kill the baby boys, but somehow Moses's life was spared. He was placed in the river in a basket. He was then saved by the daughter of a pharaoh and raised in the palace as an Egyptian prince. Moses witnessed a horrific act of injustice towards his people, the Israelis. He killed the perpetrator. Moses found himself in a place where he did the wrong thing with the wrong motive, he killed an Egyptian who was oppressing the Israelites; that caused him to leave the city and embark on a new journey. He left the region as his own life was now in danger.

Forty years later, God was sending him back on a mission. Moses had an encounter with the Lord, a moment of conviction, calling, and commissioning. Forty years prior, Moses felt a conviction to do something about the injustice that his people were experiencing, but he moved in the wrong timing using the wrong tools. However, this did not change the assignment that was evident through the conviction in his heart.

Moses's wilderness experience caused him to mature, even though he was fearful. He tried not to accept the assignment of the Lord to go to Pharaoh and deliver the children of Israel from bondage; he eventually said yes to the will of the Lord concerning him. Moses felt that he had no authority, power or the skill necessary to communicate effectively with the Egyptian establishment. In the process of receiving his calling the only thing he had to come to terms with is that he was sent by God and therefore equipped to fulfill the assignment. Moses had to realize that God could do all things, "I know that you can do all things; no purpose of yours can be thwarted" (Job 42:2). In other words, God's purpose could not be circumvented, hindered or frustrated. In Exodus 9:16 the Lord declared to Moses that He raise him up for a specific purpose. "But I have raised you up for this very purpose, that I might show you my power and that my name might be proclaimed in all the earth" (NIV).

I came to the realization that the call of God was also on my life, "He has saved us and called us to a holy life—not because of anything we have done but because of his own purpose and grace" (2 Timothy 1:9). This means a life that will bring glory and honor to the Lord, revealing Christ to others. In spite of my own desires and what I deemed as inadequacies, I felt God's compassion towards humanity, meeting the needs of others. I needed to be cognizant of the fact that I was:

- Designed
- Intentional
- Relevant
- On Point (Precise or Targeted)

In other words, I was called for this time with a specific purpose in the heart and mind of God and I was being prepared to fulfill the calling on my life. Somehow I knew that there was more to do with my life and the Lord began to put people around me to help me understand that purpose, "The purposes of a person's heart are deep waters, but one who has insight draws them out" (Proverbs 20:5). "…for it is God who works in you to will and to act in order to fulfill his good purpose" (Philippians 2:12-13). I was about to embark on one of the most exciting journeys of my life, scary, but certainly exciting. There are important aspects of my journey that demonstrate the power of God and how he can change our lives and position us to fulfill destiny. I grew up in a single parent household, but by the age of twenty-five, I was a university professor.

As a university professor in the field of social work during the 1990s, in England, I had the privilege of traveling to other universities across the world to aid in the development of their social work programs and to speak at conferences on social justice. I visited Russia, Denmark, Finland, Sweden, Germany, and America. I am now an American citizen who emigrated from the United Kingdom. I have visited India, Ghana and various Caribbean Islands on Mission trips. I have a love and an affinity for nations, culture, and people groups. My time spent traveling to various nations has shaped my thinking and how I view people and globalization. From my perspective, it appears that as a global society, we now seem to find ourselves, yet again, in a crisis; political, social, and economic leaders are making decisions that will change the trajectory of world history. I moved to America in 2000. Since then, it seems that the belief system, the interpretations of the constitution, has developed over time. I have seen political and economic polarization among social and cultural groups, with each group being passionate about ensuring that their voice is heard and that their needs are met. "The United States is in a cultural crisis. There are gaping fissures between the rich and poor, growing tensions between races, disunity among faith groups, increasing resentment between genders, and a vast and expanding gap between liberals and conservatives. Generation, gender, socioeconomics, ethnicity, faith, and politics massively divide the American population" (Barna Group, March 2016). The church, as well as the rest of society, has been affected by these challenges; healing and unity in people and groups is required in every segment of society. I do believe that it is the role of the Church, the Christ-centered community, to provide stability and direction in times of chaos and change, to navigate our nations to the next terrain of thinking, believing, and acting. As a body of Christian believers, sometimes we fail to understand that the creations of belief systems are always at work; we do not have the option to do nothing. The question now becomes, "How do we address the present crisis? And how do we get our thinking, believing, and acting processes on course to produce a harmonious, unified global community built on a biblical worldview inclusive of social justice?"

Over the past few years, I have become increasingly aware of the crisis that we are facing in our local communities and the course that America and the global community is on. As I listen to the media's responses to social and natural devastations, I hear a sense of frustration, hopelessness, and even panic among people in general. Many ask the question, "What kind of nation have we become? Why is there so much killing? How can we fix this? What will America, or the world, look like for our children, our grandchildren, and the generations to come?" These questions and more have been weighing heavily on my mind for the past few years, and I have not been able to absolve myself of the responsibility to do something about them.

There were times when I felt that, as one individual, I could not make a difference, but then the Lord reminded me that one person could make a difference. As I looked back into biblical history, I was able to see that there were several individuals that shifted the courses of their respective nations. Joseph's interpretation of the king's dream allowed an entire nation to allocate resources appropriately in preparation for a season of famine. This wisdom not only blessed Egypt, but the surrounding nations also. Secondly, Nehemiah was used instrumentally in rebuilding the walls of Jerusalem and realigning the people in terms of worship, spirituality, and cultural values. The Lord reminded me that what He requires us to do would certainly make a difference; we simply have to trust the Lord and move according to His timing. I believe that the Lord is raising up a generation of visionaries who will make a difference—those who will have the faith, boldness, and tenacity to implement the will and word of God in their communities.

Our nation is in need of healing; the people are looking for solutions that will bring peace and security. The Scriptures declare in Psalm 1 that as a believer in God, we are trees planted by the rivers of water and our source of hope is in the living God. As a tree, the church is required to produce leaves of healing for our nations (Revelation 22:2). The phrase "leaves of healing" means that what we produce as a group of visionaries or leaders should bring relief, stability, healing, and growth for our nations.

Contrary to popular belief or what may appear to be a negative time for some individuals, this is an exciting time for the Church to be active, productive and bring God glory. I truly believe that this present chaos is going to produce the order that is necessary for future generations. People are being courageous and strong and are not afraid to take a stand for righteousness and justice. The Holman Bible declares that the Lord "loves righteousness and justice; the earth is full of the LORD's unfailing love (Psalm 33:5). And that "the LORD executes acts of righteousness and justice for all the oppressed" (Psalm 103:6). It is critical as a nation to walk in both righteousness and justices for the blessings over the nation to be released. We can see this biblical principle with Abraham in Genesis 18:19, "For I know him, that he will command his children and his household after him, and they shall keep the way of the LORD, to do justice and judgment; that the LORD may bring upon Abraham that which he hath spoken of him." We need the promises and the blessings released over America, the United Kingdom, and every nation that is seeking the face of the Lord Jesus Christ.

With every power shift, there is a power surge; in other words, often, those that hold the power will determine legislation. While in prayer, I heard that we are going to see multijurisdictional cooperation across the Body of Christ, with churches and groups supporting one another like never before. In my observation and talking to different leaders in the Christian world, people are ready to focus on commonalties and work together, rather than let our differences keep them segregated. If change is to occur, we must realize that we need one another; each church or individual carries different anointings and gifts that were never meant to operate in isolation. The scriptures declare that "From whom the whole body fitly joined together and compacted by that which every joint supplieth, according to the effectual working in the measure of every part, maketh increase of the body unto the edifying of itself in love (Ephesians 4:16)". We can no longer operate in isolation, disjointed and alienated from each other. We must recognize we can no longer debate which organization; ministry, business or leader is the greatest. We cannot allow the enemy to continue to have an advantage over us while we are in disunity, our focus has to be laser sharp, focused on clarity, direction and solutions on God's plan and will for our nations. In this season, we are shifting from crying about carrying our cross (Matthew 16:24) to learning how to operate with our thorn in our side (2 Corinthians 12:7–9). We are coming to the realization that there is power beyond the cross. The thorn simply reminds us to remain humble and that God's grace is sufficient to keep us where He takes us; we must be consistent, persistent, and relentless.

We are in an exciting era of leadership, there are some faith-based leaders who are shifting from titles and a shifting to a role of operation and demonstration; leaders who will dare to believe God for the impossible. I have spoken to many leaders who occupy the seven mountains or seven spheres of cultural influence: the church, family, education, politics, media, arts and entertainment, and economy. The term the seven mountains of influence was developed in 1975 by Bill Bright, founder of Campus Crusade, and Loren Cunningham, founder of Youth With a Mission (YWAM) as a strategy to bring godly change to a nation (Generals international, 2016). These leaders across the nations concur that there is kingdom reassignment taking place, and we believe that this is the period that will make a significant impact in history. There is a group of emerging leaders waiting in the wings, ready to give birth to the plans of God in the earth realm. With the death of an old era, something new and fresh comes forth.

In this book, I will share with you my personal story and the concepts and principles that the Lord has taught me concerning how to birth a vision. I am the senior pastor of Shiloh Worship Center, located in the rural area of Belton, Texas. Our church has been on a journey since its inception in 2002, and as a leader, I have come to realize that personal preparation and sacrifices are critical to the success of any visionary. Our foundation in Christ or our belief systems must be our strong foundation if we aim to build a sturdy vision or structure. What God has called us to do will sometimes cause us to face challenges and even opposition; we must be able to stand the test of time in what we believe and what we have heard from the Lord.

I have experienced days of great success, as well as days of epic failures. I do believe I have learned some phenomenal lessons that need to be shared. These lessons will bring enlightenment to every visionary—those in the church as well as those operating in the corporate world, marketplace leaders. No matter what area of ministry we occupy, personal preparation will precede operation; we must yield our time, talents, and gifts to the Lord or to the organization and organism that we serve. To be released in our kingdom assignment, a kingdom alignment must take place.

The book is divided into two parts. Part one deals with the concept of FIRST. Before we can enter the season of birthing a vision, there are several stages that we will go through. The revelation of FIRST is an authentic and exciting analysis based on my own journey. FIRST means *Forgiveness, from Baali to Ishi, Raising Kingdom Seeds, Subpoenaed by Heaven,* and *The* Process.

- **F**orgiveness
- **I**shi
- **R**aising kingdom seeds
- **S**ubpoenaed by heaven
- **T**he Process

Part one will deal with some very important concepts that will encourage you to both endure and enjoy the journey that will involve birthing the vision, imparting the vision, and dealing with vision blockers. These concepts are not dealt with in the order presented above; instead, it was necessary to address the concepts based on chronological experience.

Once we have been personally developed and processed, the heart of a visionary will begin to emerge within us. Part two begins with discussing the heart that a visionary is required to cultivate to ensure success. This section then focuses on pioneering the vision and identifies how this can be accomplished. Finally, part two provides a practical framework for developing a vision in which I provide an extensive analysis of a Brilliant Business Model.

This book is intriguing and exciting, providing you with practical tools to ensure victories in terms of vision development. The vision emergence template (VET) that I offer is an excellent resource, and you will be equipped to run with whatever God has given you, regardless of the industry you may operate in. The conclusion is awe-inspiring; you will find declarations that you can speak over the vision, which will bring life during the process, after the process, and for years to come.

The book is designed to reduce the increasing rate of aborted and abandoned visions, dreams, and hopes. The Scripture declares, "Where there is no vision, the people perish: but he that keepeth the law, happy is he" (Proverbs 29:18). A clearly defined vision is the legislative framework in which one should operate; it is the law established by the Lord for the vision to be realized by the visionary. I declare that after reading this book, you will not perish and you will no longer be detached from the will of God concerning you. You will be strengthened and encouraged to walk in the divine plan of God, His command for you, in your due season, in your "now" season. The Bible clearly states that blessings are released over us and over our environments when we obey the Lord.

Part One

The Birth of a Vision

Shall I bring to the birth, and not cause to bring forth?
saith the LORD: shall I cause to bring forth, and shut
the womb? saith thy God.

—Isaiah 66:9

Chapter 1

Subpoenaed by Heaven

As I began to come to a state of consciousness about my existence as a spiritual being in the earth realm, I also began to realize that I had been trying to smother the voice of God in my life. I believed the lies of the enemy and had become a perverted version of what God was calling me to be. I once heard a powerful man of God teach about Joseph, the favorite son of Jacob (Genesis 37); he stated that when there is a calling on your life, you could sometimes become a shadow or a perversion of God's intentions. I was content for a season with my accomplishments in the secular world. It was truly epic to be a twenty-five-year-old female of color teaching in a university setting in a predominantly rural area in England during the early nineties. The favor of God was on my life, and He allowed the doors to be open, but that was not the complete plan of God concerning me.

I was in a season where God was disturbing my sleep; it started a journey of questioning my existence and purpose. It was at that point that my spirit began to open up to being in tune with the voice and the will of God. I knew the call of God was on my life when I was a little girl. The Lord spoke to me at the age of six and said nothing could hurt me unless I believed that it could. I had a passion for God in my teenage years. As I grew up, somehow allowed the disappointments of life to slowly close down my sensitivity to the voice of God, allowing life issues to hurt and hinder my walk with the Lord.

During my early twenties, I was served with a writ and commanded to attend the courts of heaven. The text convicted my heart; no matter where I turned in the Word, which is God, He was speaking directly to me. The Word of God became a "written authoritative command," and I started looking at the word of God in a different way; it became more personal and alive in my life than ever before. I felt the Spirit of the Lord calling me higher. I believe at some point, every believer is subpoenaed by heaven, but the question is "What do we do with it?" At one point in time, I tried to ignore it and run from it. I made all kinds of excuses. *God could not be talking to me*, I thought. I felt that my life was a wreck with no possible recovery. I was in the midst of a broken marriage, embarking on a journey of single parenthood; I failed to recognize that God specialized in the impossible. I was so focused on what was going right that I neglected to see the things in my life that was failing until it was broken. The very thing that I feared was the very thing that I now had to face; I came from a broken home and did not want my daughters to go through the same experience.

The Lord then reminded me about how He called the apostle Peter from his secular job. The skills, experience, and discipline gained from the secular arena were necessary for how the Lord would use him in the spiritual. I was a university professor in social work and sociology for ten years; through that profession, the Lord developed three main areas in my life:

1. *Research*

    I understood the importance of researching to ensure that the information and knowledge that would be shared with a group was accurate. I also learned the necessary skills to be a teacher. The Lord developed this area of anointing, teaching me how to unlock the Word prophetically.

2. *Leadership Development*

    I supervised students during their placements, and the Lord developed the compassion that I needed to develop and raise up effective leaders in the kingdom; I developed the necessary skills and patience in this area.

3. *Intercession for Nations*

As an international liaison for the university, I traveled to many countries: Denmark, Sweden, Germany, Russia, Finland, and the United States. It was during those times in my hotel room by myself that I learned how to intercede for a nation. I had very little understanding back then, but I would enquire of the Lord concerning why He brought me to those countries and what He wanted me to do; I would lie on the floor in my hotel room and pray for these nations.

Like the Apostle Peter, there was a call to discipleship, to be a follower of Jesus Christ, and to promote the move of the kingdom. I was being taught how to walk in the fivefold ministry. I was called to evangelize my community; I saw my assignment as helping to prepare the believers of Christ to take dominion of the earth. There was a time when I too failed to respond to the voice of God due to my fears of failure and rejection, but I heard the Scripture in my spirit saying, "And the Lord said, Simon, Simon, behold, Satan hath desired to have you, that he may sift you as wheat: But I have prayed for thee, that thy faith fail not: and when thou art converted, strengthen thy brethren" (Luke 22:31–32). The Lord showed me the following through this Scripture:

- Jesus had a plan for Simon, who was also known as Peter.
- The Lord was able see Peter's potential in spite of his faults.
- The Lord was able to use Peter's weakness as strength.
- Jesus still sent a word to Peter even after he denied the Lord.
- Although Peter felt badly and wept bitterly, he was able to pull himself together and answer the call. Peter's relationship with Christ was secure enough that Peter could receive forgiveness and not wallow in his sorrow.
- When Peter came to himself and arrived at his position for destiny, he was commissioned by the Lord.

I was comfortable with my life, even if it was broken; I somehow learnt how to block the pain of hurt and disappointment. But I did not want to surrender the life I knew, my comfort zone, for that which was unknown. It is imperative for us as believers to remember that Jesus already knows our weaknesses and failures. Based on our revelation of who Jesus is, we already have received the keys to the kingdom, the promises of God, a future of good and not evil. We came into the earth realm on time and with purpose. The assignment, our purpose, and destiny were established before the foundation of the world. "For I know the thoughts that I think toward you, saith the LORD, thoughts of peace, and not of evil, to give you an expected end" (Jeremiah 29:11).

During the process of moving into the perfect will of God and being prepared to possess the promise, we can sometimes begin to believe that God does not care about us, especially when He does not respond to our demands (not prayers, but demands). The fact is that God does care about us, and He has taken the time to allow the things in our lives that are hindering us from walking in our calling to dissipate or die. I soon discovered that if I truly wanted to please God and be in His perfect will; I could no longer run from the calling on my life. Boldness comes through the Holy Ghost, and it was time to let the Spirit of God have full dominion in my life. It was time for me to be a witness, give evidence, and testify of the transforming power of the blood of Jesus. The Lord was challenging me to no longer be a bystander; this was the open door to ministry that I had told God I was ready, willing, and able to walk through. Peter was, at one time, a bystander who denied Christ multiple times, and like Peter, I eventually had to take my foot out the doors of the past and stop weeping. I discovered that there was a way back from denying Christ that led to becoming one of His reliable, credible witnesses. This happened when I accepted the will of God for my life in the mid-1990s.

Have you ever been at a point in your life where everything appears to be going well, you have accomplished the goals that you have set for yourself and you are finally financially established, but there is no peace and contentment in your heart and mind? There is still a void that all your accomplishments could not fill. In the year

1993, I found myself in such a position. My children were young, ages four and five. I had grown up in a single-parent household and knew the associated struggles of being a single parent and the importance of accomplishment. I completed my bachelor's degree while pregnant with my second child and was well on my way to completing my master's in the summer of 1994. Not knowing what to expect from marriage, I thought that I had accomplished the best that I could in life: I was married with two adorable daughters, a house, and two cars. Then why couldn't I sleep at night? Tossing and turning, with no peace, I felt the hand of God touching my heart. I heard His voice calling me from a distance. It was then that I recalled all the promises I had made to God as a child. I remember distinctly at the age of six years old that I wanted to get baptized in water in the name of Jesus, but my father felt that I was too young. I was raised under strong apostolic leadership; my pastor, Bishop Herman D. Brown, nurtured my heart to hear the voice of God. I remember my mother praying under very difficult circumstances, and I knew then that Jesus was truly the answer to life's woes, as well as a loving father and the God of blessings and provision. Through good times and bad times, the Name of Jesus had power in my home.

I remember in my early teens that the spirit of revival broke out in our church. All of the young people were at the altar seeking the infilling of the Holy Ghost. I wanted Him so desperately to come and dwell in me, to overtake me. It did not matter how long it took; we were seeking the Lord at the altar many days into the night hours, seeking the face of God. Our pastor and the praying mothers and fathers set the atmosphere for Jesus to come and saturate the house with His glory, and we experienced the drunkenness of the outpouring of the Holy Spirit. Back then, I did not fully understand what God was doing, but the Lord Jesus was establishing Himself in me. I remember having such a thirst for the Lord in my teens; I would study my Bible for hours.

How did I forget this relationship that I had with Jesus? I had an excellent mother, but somehow she could not fill the void of an absent father who abandoned his baby girl, his little lamb, as he would call me. My father walked away from the Lord when I was a baby, and by the age of nine, my father walked away from the Lord and his family. It would be thirty-six years later when I would see my father again, but that's another story for another time. I walked away from my love relationship with the Lord in my early twenties. I thought that marrying, even if it were outside of the perfect will of God, would make me happy, but the true happiness that I was looking for was not in the temporal things. Eventually, I woke up and came to myself.

I remember one of the mothers in the ministry came to me and shared a vision that the Lord had given her concerning me. The Lord showed her that I would be teaching groups of women around the world at various conferences and events. When this vision was shared with me, I was young, and I was in a marriage with a husband that did not believe in women operating in ministry. My question to God was, "How are you going to do this?" I can't say I had the Mary experience when she found out that she was pregnant with Jesus, "How shall this be" (Luke 1:34). I simply said to myself that this was not possible; I was not positioned for the vision that was given to me. I had established my identity in my job. The Lord had shown me great favor and success, and I was teaching in a university by the age of twenty-five. I did not feel that I was qualified to handle spiritual matters. Although I was in the church, I had walked away from God in my late teenage years to my early twenties; I abandoned my Christian values for a season. I knew better but did not do what was right, so I told myself that God could not want to use me. I realized that I was still carrying the shame of my past. Although the Lord Jesus and others had forgiven me, I had not forgiven myself. The shame of the past overshadowed the promise of my future; I thought that I had altered the course of my destiny and that I had reached the point of no return.

Why am I writing this testimony? As a leader, I have come to realize that my life is an open book; although I was in a household, where I saw my biological father abuse my mother and brother from a young age, I had no excuse for walking out of the will of God concerning me. I did not allow God to minister to my hurting places and my insecurities. Looking back over my life, I was really successful in some areas, such as academically, and failed miserably in other areas of my life, such as relationships. I was loved and validated by my mother, but although my father did not physically abuse me, I was terrified by his presence. The Apostle Paul tells us in 2 Corinthians 3:2, "Ye are our epistle written in our hearts, known and read of all men." I should have been the product of a God-fearing upbringing. I was instructed in the Word by my mother but somehow did not have the will or the strength to walk in the Word; my fleshly desires became my god, my first priority. When you take your focus off the Lord Jesus Christ, you subject yourself to the laws of nature. The scriptures tells us, "For all that is in the world, the lust of the flesh, and the lust of the eyes, and the pride of life, is not of the Father, but is of the world" (1 John 2:16). I walked in the lust of my flesh, and I was prideful of my achievements. There is no good thing in the flesh, and it can only be annihilated by the power of the Holy Spirit, the divine nature of God. We cannot live in two camps and abide by two different sets of laws; one will eventually take precedence over the other. The Apostle Paul expresses this clearly in the Word of God; we have two natures fighting against each other, and they are contrary, they conflict, and they are complete opposites of each other. Depending on which nature is fed the most (the strong man), either the flesh or the Spirit will determine what decisions we will make in our lives. I have since been delivered from my fears of the role of a father and have been able to tell my story. I realize that my heavenly father was not a bully who reigned with tyranny. He was loving, forgiving, and compassionate toward me, even in my faults and failures. The scriptures became life, "When my father and my mother forsake me, then the LORD will take me up" (Psalms 27:10). I was set up for success, I learnt how to be a loving parent through my mother, my heavenly father, and later, through my God-given father, my stepdad.

By the end of 1993, there was a yearning in my spirit to find out my purpose and destiny. On the first Sunday of 1994, one of the elders, who were one of the leaders at Mount Shiloh Church Wolverhampton, England, my home church, which I grew up in, preached the Word of the Lord. I felt like the Word was specifically targeted at me; somehow, I felt like the only person sitting in the church. I remember he preached that there was a storm coming and that our lives would never be the same again. I was married, I had my two beautiful little girls. As someone who had experienced abandonment from her biological father as a child and had watched her mother struggle to raise children, these accomplishments were extremely important, but there was so much more for me to accomplish. I limited myself to what I thought I could achieve.

I did not realize at that time how much growing up without a loving father affected me. I was dealing with the spirit of abandonment, which affected my decision making in my early adult life. Because I had experienced an emotional tearing away of a father figure, a life source, which was supposed to validate me, it was easy for me to give up quickly during adverse challenges in my role as a leader. To abandon means to give up to the control or influence of something or a person. Abandonment can cause you to sabotage your own destiny because you do not feel worthy of what God is saying about your life. Some individuals who have experienced abandonment like myself may find it easy to withdraw from others, especially when we feel that we are facing danger. It is easy to give up with the intent of never again claiming a right or interest in something that was given to us, or something that we were supposed to accomplish. We can get into the mode of protecting ourselves so that we don't feel the original pain of loss and separation; if something were challenging me in relationships with others, I did not want to deal with it.

Abandonment tears things and people that you love away from you, so it can sometimes lead you to hold on to things tightly even if they are not good for you. You can also end up entertaining the spirit of abandonment and withdrawing yourself from life or situations that you have no control over; it is difficult to walk in faith when you entertain this spirit; in other words, you may be surrounded by love, but we cannot see it due to past hurts. We can make our past experiences a present reality. When a person withdraws their presence and support from another person or organization, reneges on their responsibilities, and betrays covenant or commitment, this is called abandonment. The enemy seduces people, particularly those who play a key role in the life of another person or an organization's development and progress, to renege on commitments and contracts and to walk away from relationships and responsibilities. This act of abdication has the power and ability to cause great emotional pain, spiritual misalignment, financial hardship, organizational chaos, and confusion in the abandoned individual.

The issue of abandonment was my main hindrance in developing a vision. I had to be healed and be whole to push forward into uncharted territory and successfully birth a vision that will bring life to a region. We all experience different or similar roadblock to us birthing a vision; abandonment was mine. I understand that abandonment leaves you wounded at the "soul level." It hurts you at your very core, tearing at your heart and mind. Your psyche or mental health is disturbed, to say the least, and very often, the foundations of your beliefs are shaken. But sometimes destiny is trying to get us into our place of purpose; we cannot allow our past to hinder our future. I could not allow the issues that accompany abandonment to plague me, issues such as the following:

1. The inability to trust others

2. Suspicion

3. The spirit of manipulation

4. Shame and despondency

5. Fear of rejection

6. Loneliness or isolation

7. Codependency on others

We have to identify our hurting places and roadblocks to be healed, to ensure success for our future. It becomes very dangerous when we become self-centered, focused on our disappointments; this does not allow us to focus on the perfect will of God concerning you. Although I had friends, I felt different and somewhat inferior because of the lack of a father. It did not matter that some of my friends' fathers were dysfunctional, drunks, abusers, or gamblers; the fact is they had a father. At that time, I did not realize that I was allowing the enemy to play with my mind. We can be in the house of God but still feel lonely and lost; we must address our low self-esteem and a lack of self-worth, if we are experiencing these concerns. It's interesting how the issues in our lives can appear polarized at times; we can be at different ends of the confidence equilibrium at the same time. That in itself can be a dichotomy, posing a conflict in our psyche.

Having a family and being able to provide for my family was my primary concern. I did not want to struggle or my children to experience lack. During the preached word on that first Sunday in January 1994, the Lord began to talk to me. I tried to create my own destiny, which was out of the perfect will of God. My idea of my future was to raise my children and focus on my career, meeting the needs of others was not in my mind's eye. I soon realized that I couldn't ask to be in the will of God without expecting something in my life to change. Alignment is going to cost you something; it is a move from one place to the next and a state of agreement and cooperation with the Lord's will for my life. I had to reevaluate my dreams and goals and embark on a new course of learning. This was to become the season where I was going to be trained for ministry and see this as a privilege to serve the people of God and my community.

I have found that a lot of great leaders have overcome some difficult experiences; this is often what makes them great. To lead effectively, we have to address our wounds very early in leadership. As pioneers, we will experience wounds often as we cut through the thicket and make paths that others can follow. We cannot withdraw our presence and support from another person or organization and renege on our duties, responsibilities, and obligations; we cannot betray our covenants or commitments to what we have been called to do.

During that same year, I felt like a tornado hit my life, which led to a change in my family structure and functioning. By the end of that year, I was a single parent. The next year, my pastor called me to work with the administrative team. I felt like a broken mess and wondered why he would want me to help with anything at the church. I had nothing to offer, so I thought. The church had a strong administrative team, which I was happy to assist with in whatever capacity they needed me. I somehow ended up spending time weekly with my pastor, paying bills, and replying to any correspondence mailed to the church. I soon realized that it was not about what I had to offer, but more importantly what I needed to learn.

I remember I felt the need to reduce my work hours from full-time to four days a week so that I could sit at my pastor's feet every Monday. Working in the church administrative office ended up being more than paying bills, responding to correspondence, making appointments, etc.; those next four years would change my life forever. He saw in me what I did not see in myself. Sometimes, I was there for hours as we talked, and I gleaned wisdom. My pastor would tell me about my biological father; he was a powerful minister of the gospel who stood head and shoulders above his peers, and he was an intellectual that had a profound teaching anointing and a calling for leadership. As a young child, I did not get to experience that side of my father; he stopped going to church when I was a toddler and moved away when I was nine years old. As a child, I was fearful of his behavior toward his family. Unfortunately, although he was gifted, my father did not know how to deal with his generational curses; he saw his father abuse his mother and reproduced that behavior in his own marriage.

As I write this book, I now realize that I was going through my healing process and understanding my generational anointing and blessings. My pastor fathered me and would call me one of his daughters; I was offered the opportunity to change the trajectory of my life. It was in those years that my pastor was developing my identity and enlightening my understanding in terms of my gifting and my purpose. At that time, I had no idea what the Lord had planned for my life, but I had a leader who could see beyond my present circumstance, my place of pain, brokenness, shame, and embarrassment. My pastor prepared me and propelled me to my destiny. I was thirty years old when this process started; we are never too old to begin healing. I realized there was a deeper meaning to my life and my purpose in the earth. I had options. I first had to know my blessings and promise in order to access and activate them.

Two years later, my pastor called me on a Saturday and told me that I would be preaching during the morning service the next day—less than twenty-four hours' notice. I was in shock and began sobbing on the phone, hoping that somehow my tears would absolve me of this obligation. Well, it did not. My pastor told me to be myself and bring whatever God gave me, even if it was only ten minutes. I was being stretched beyond my comfort zone; my *then* was preparing me for my *now*.

At the beginning of April 1998, the Lord reminded me that everything that I had gone through and accomplished was to bring me to a place where I could publish with the voice of thanksgiving the goodness of our Lord Jesus Christ and tell of all His wondrous works (Psalm 26:7). The Lord would talk to me like a friend and a lover. The key was to stay daily in prayer, asking God for protection for what was in me; I had to guard the treasures within. The Lord is our protector, and He promised to walk before me in the land of the living; His glory and power were my shield and buckler, my covering and my rear guard. The Lord reminded me to hold on to what He has given me. He told me that during the making process, many lose their keys, the power to loose and bind. It is imperative to stay in our places of anointing and empowerment, in spite of what it may look like around us. When God speaks, His word is established and settled in the heavens, waiting for fulfillment in the earth.

During my period of transition and change, the Lord ministered to me through Psalm 26. The Lord would judge me, execute everything in me that was not like God, and examine, prove, and shape my heart before He could trust me with His heart. The Lord had to "try my reins," renew my mind, my feeling, and affections, and heal my heart of all hurt, bitterness, and un-forgiveness. I had to change my associations and learn to love the house of the Lord.

Integrity was a key component in this next chapter of my life. It was essential to walk uprightly before the Lord in order to release the anointing necessary to fulfill destiny and purpose. It was also essential to know the Word of God, God Himself, to be complete and whole in Him.

The Lord gave me specific instructions that would propel me to my next place in God:

> Do not let anyone tell you that you are not healed; you are healed. Stay in your prayer closet because flesh will try to destroy you. God has a ministry in you that the world needs, but it is all in my timing. Learn to walk with the footman. Do not walk before or behind God; stay under the covering of God, and He will teach you how to run with the horseman. It's time to write; incorporate all your experiences. You have learned how to appease God, touch His heart, and love Him. I have called you into the nation of America. Do not be concerned about your finances; there is a home already prepared for you. You will minister to kings and generals. The Lord has honored your sacrifice and your children will be blessed; they will be pearls at your side. The ministry is going to grow beyond your wildest imagination. Fear not and stay humble. (The Lord Jesus, April 24, 1998)

The Lord shared so much during the preparation process, some of which has yet to come to pass. We have to be careful not to speak anything before its time; it can be misunderstood or the enemy can seek to destroy the fulfillment of the promise.

A dear friend told me that I had to learn to ride the crest of the waves; each wave would take me closer to my destiny. The waves would roar and the sea would not always be still, but it was essential to remember that God was in control of everything. To ensure the mercies and protection of the Lord, I had to be in right standing with Him, striving for perfection continually.

It was thirty-six years later that I would see my father again, in 2011, when He was sick. He had the onset of dementia and prostate cancer. He could remember who I was at times. I was grateful that I was healed; he was unable to validate who I was, but I was able to validate whom he was—loved, forgiven, and honored as a life source. I ended up preaching at my father's funeral three years later in his home community in Jamaica.

Naked and Unashamed

Every leader and every visionary will face times of discouragement. Sometimes we have to get "naked and unashamed" with God for the healing process to begin. The Lord already knows where we are spiritually and what condition our heart is in. There was a season in which my mother, who is an awesome intercessor, told me to write a "Dear God" letter; writing this letter would help to direct me in prayer, as it would expose the condition of my heart. Jeremiah 17:9 reads, "The heart is deceitful above all things, and desperately wicked: who can know it?" My mother taught me that prayer is effective and effectual and that it can bring about change, a refreshing, a renewing, and revival. I wrote my letter.

> Dear God,
>
> I am so grateful for life, health, and strength. I know the right thing to do is to acknowledge You and glorify You above all else before I start talking about me, and before I start my complaint. My heart is so overwhelmed with grief, I FEEL a deep sense of loss and failure. I am wondering why you have me here, in what I feel like is a God-forsaken place, among a people where the majority do not even like or respect me. God, I have done all I can do at this point, and I am trying not to faint with a weariness of heart. I know if I give in, I will never recover. God, I am so lost. I do not understand my purpose anymore, or if it is worth fighting for the vision. Lord, I am tired and wounded. I have been beaten, spat upon, ridiculed, and talked about. I feel the spirits in the region pushing me to go home and leave this place; never to return. I feel the disgust; sometimes I don't even know how to raise my head. There are times I feel that I can never get it right; I please no one, not even You or me! What am I doing here? What is my assignment? Even those that live a Godless life and a life that lacks integrity walk over me. Am I being punished for the sins of my youth? Failure

and disappointment seem to be my portion. I know I am not the victim, but I am sure in a lot of pain!

I feel hate and scorned in this region; somehow You cause me to keep lifting my head up, even when I want to hang it down and walk in shame. You cause me to leave the house, even when I want to stay in a fetal position in a corner in the dark. You cause me to hope beyond hope, even though my dreams are deferred. Somehow You keep me connected to Your heart when I want to give up. The umbilical cord is feeding me when I don't have the strength to go on. You send me little reminders of the prophetic words, phone calls, and encouragement from those that You have placed in my life to keep me from falling. But right now, somehow, this does not seem like enough; it does not make the pain go away.

I am so hurt. How did I get to this place of abandonment? Why have the people that I loved and care for rejected me? You told me to serve You in Spirit and in Truth. You told me to cry, "Holy"; I did that. Lord, you told me to lift up a standard; I did that. I have loved your people in the time of their brokenness; and the moment they get well, they turn on me. Very few say, "Thank you"; they smile at me while the knife is in my back. Through all this, I know that you are God. I know you are alive and well.

I then stopped writing; I was able to see how deceptive the voice of the enemy was in the midst of transition and the birthing of a vision. I was having, what I call, an Elijah moment: "But he himself went a day's journey into the wilderness, and came and sat down under a juniper tree: and he requested for himself that he might die; and said, It is enough; now, O LORD, take away my life; for I am not better than my fathers" (1 Kings 19:4). Hopelessness and despair are real emotions that leaders go through, but they must be dealt with immediately in prayer and by seeking Godly counsel; we cannot focus on the deception of the flesh, our feelings. My Elijah moment came through the wound of abandonment; you may experience something

DR. CLAUDETTE MORGAN-SCOTT

different but equally as painful or debilitating. You cannot afford to have a "woe is me pity party." That kind of party is way too expensive, uninviting, and dull; you lose a lot in the process. It is imperative that you have people in your life who are godly and wise, people you can trust with your heart. You need someone with whom you can be "naked and unashamed," someone who will not judge you but will pour the oil of healing on your brokenness. The enemy's intention is to influence you to give up on the plan of God concerning both you and the people that God has put in your life. After waking up from self-pity, I soon realized that so many leaders get into this place and either give up or sometimes even commit spiritual, emotional, or natural suicide. I declare right now if you are struggling with any of these emotions, that your deliverance, healing, and hope is coming now, in the name of Jesus; you shall rise and live again!

From My Baali to My Ishi

And it shall be at that day, saith the LORD, that thou shalt call me Ishi; and shalt call me no more Baali.

—Hosea 2:16

Becoming a single parent was devastating. I so desperately wanted my girls to experience what I did not have: the joy of having a father in the home. In the midst of distress and crying in the night season, I had to learn who God was to me. Knowing about God was essential, but it was time to know Him for myself. As a single parent, it was a struggle to stay focused on the things of the kingdom. Sometimes I felt so overwhelmed that I did not even know if I could make it. I could not see where I was going. There were times when the pain seemed unbearable. The questions began to emerge, and the accuser was right there, speaking in my ear:

- You are a failure.
- You are unlovable.
- You don't deserve to be loved.

- God can't keep you from falling.
- Everyone is embarrassed for you.
- Look at you; you're a mess!
- And on and on…

Lies, lies, and more lies continued to be spewed from the voice of the enemy. We have to be careful which voice we listen to; the enemy, the flesh, or the voice of the Lord. The Lord took me into the book of Hosea later in my journey, and He began to reveal Himself to me. The name of the Old Testament prophet Hosea means "salvation," and he was a type and shadow of Jesus Christ. The Hebrew definition of the name Hosea also means "to free, avenge, defend, preserve, and rescue." No matter how many times our sins or circumstances separate us from God, He is on a mission to deliver His seeds of righteousness from the hand of the adversary.

Deliverance from the hand of the enemy was not because there was any good in me, but it was based on the righteousness of God; because of His sinless nature, Jesus could have dominion over my strongholds. Hosea was an Old Testament prophet who was instructed by the Lord to marry a wife who had the reputation of being a prostitute. The life of Hosea and his wife was a typology of the life of God and His relationship and his chosen people, the nation of Israel. The children of Israel had strayed away from the Lord and worshiped the gods of other nations; Gomer's relationship with Hosea was filled with betrayal and adultery. Hosea did not divorce her but took her back every time she returned to him. I was able to identify with Gomer in this situation; I had strayed away from the Lord, in my heart, time after time, even though I knew that I had a calling on my life. I had failed to believe that He had a perfect plan for me and that His Word over me was "yea and amen," sealed until the day of redemption. I had set myself up as an idol, formulating and executing these grand pity parties: "Why me, Lord? It's not fair! I will not be able to survive this, God!" Oh, how foolish I was. It was time for me to bring an end to my failures and stop protecting the things that did not concern God. I had to recognize that certain negative things had been produced in me that I needed to address. Gomer had three children with Hosea in the midst of her sleeping with other men, whose names were as follows:

Child	Definition
Jezreel (son)	God will sow, disseminate, plant, bring forth, or conceive a seed
Loruhamah (daughter)	Not pitied, not loved, no mercy
Lo-ammi (son)	Not my people

The Lord showed me that if I stayed in His will, the seed produced would be protected and productive; my lack of commitment to God's plan for me did not alter His love for me.

The mind is very complex, consisting of cognitive faculties, which enable a state of thinking, perception, consciousness, learning, reasoning, and judgment. How we perceive the world around us will influence our decision-making and how we interact with others. Voices aid in the process of interpretation and perception. The enemy battles for the mind, but the Scriptures declare in Philippians 2:5, "Let this mind be in you, which was also in Christ Jesus."

The question then became which word I was going to receive: the word that the Lord spoke in my spirit or the subsequent words that the enemy would use to render the plan of God powerless in my life. I was a child of God, I was loved, and God would use my testimony to bless others and advance the kingdom of God. It was imperative that I receive the inheritance and blessings of the firstborn— the inheritance and blessing that the Old Testament fathers normally pronounce of their eldest child, wherein the eldest son would get a double portion of their father's inheritance (Deuteronomy 21:17). The blessing determined headship and took place prior to the death of the individual pronouncing the blessing. If I yielded my life, my spirit, my soul (my mind, my will, my emotions, my imagination, and my conscience), and my body to the Lord, then the Lord would turn my life in a direction that would please Him. My existence was about to have some meaning; I was about to discover my God-given purpose. The word of God spoken over my life was a blessing, and

I was equipped to walk in that path. It was then that I understood the words of the Lord: "Verily, verily, I say unto you, except a corn of wheat fall into the ground and die, it abideth alone: but if it dies, it bringeth forth much fruit" (John 12:24). My present perception of my life had to die for God to conceive something new in me. I had to move from a place of pain to an understanding that process leads to purpose. I was not pliable or able to extend my reach in my present form. I had to fall to the ground, dust to dust, and die; everything fleshly had to go back to the earth because it had no place in the kingdom. I had to learn to ascend to the height that the Lord was showing me in my heart, my spirit-man; I had to be made over again. I had to move from pain to purpose. I described pain and purpose in the following way:

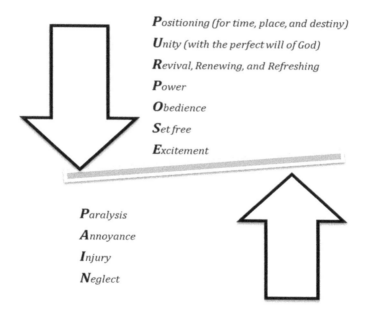

*P*ositioning *(for time, place, and destiny)*
*U*nity *(with the perfect will of God)*
*R*evival, Renewing, and Refreshing
*P*ower
*O*bedience
*S*et free
*E*xcitement

*P*aralysis
*A*nnoyance
*I*njury
*N*eglect

I could no longer be rendered subject to the pain of life. I researched the uses for corn after the crushing or processing, and I came to realize that humans or animals couldn't digest corn in its original form. Processed corn, on the other hand, has many uses: medicinal, energy (gas and oil), food, sugar, alcohol, etc. The process is necessary for productivity and purpose.

What was God doing in my life? To survive this process, I had to change my perception of God. I was not going through trouble or distress because I had done something wrong; it was so God could be glorified in me and through me. I already knew the Lord as my *Baali*, or my master, Jehovah, but for me to walk through this process successfully, God introduced Himself as my *Ishi*, or my husband, my champion, my man. The terms *Baali* and *Ishi* came from the book of Hosea as the Lord talked about the redemption of the Israel back into their place of prominence. The scriptures declare, "And it shall be at that day, saith the LORD, that thou shalt call me Ishi; and shalt call me no more Baali" (Hosea 2:16). The Lord was to be great and mighty in my life. With Jesus at my side, I was assured of His headship and leadership in my life. The Lord Jesus was now responsible for me, and I could trust His leading along the path that He would walk me through. Jesus would be my companion; He would care for me, love me, nurture me, provide for me, encourage me, and motivate me. Jesus would meet the needs of His wife and family, and we were now in a safe place to grow and mature in the things of God.

I had to allow God to take His rightful position, both in my life and in the lives of my girls, as He moved from my Master to my Husband. The Scriptures declare that the "woman's desire shall be to her husband" (Genesis 3:16), and I had a newfound love for the Lord. The Lord loved me and showed me what a husband should be like. He often showed His love and compassion through others who ministered life and hope to me.

The Process

Behold, I will do a new thing; now it shall spring forth; shall ye not know it? I will even make a way in the wilderness, and rivers in the desert.

—Isaiah 43:19

The Lord helped me understand that I would go through some difficult experiences at the beginning of the journey, but He reassured me that He would guide my path; I would not die during the journey.

Jesus prepared me for the process. The Lord took me to the scripture that says, "Neither do men put new wine into old bottles: else the bottles break, and the wine runneth out, and the bottles perish: but they put new wine into new bottles, and both are preserved" (Matthew 9:17); a transformation, new thing, and a new mind-set was going to be developed. The scriptures declare, "Behold, I will do a new thing" (Isaiah 43:19). Although this scripture was written in the Old Testament, the twenty-first-century church has used the phrase to indicate that change is on the horizon. I believe that the church is rising to the dawning of a new level of power; it is the dawning of a new day, and the true church, the church within the church, is clearly aware that God is about to do something exciting, something that we have never seen before in our lifetimes. It is not business as usual, and God needs vessels to move through.

What is this new thing? It is a new and fuller application of the principles of the Word of God that will assist us in reaching our generation, our communities, our nation, and the world at large. The Word does not change and will never change. Jesus said, "Heaven and earth shall pass away, but my word shall not pass away" (Matthew 24:35). God desires that the Church, the blood-bought saints, fully access all of His promises. God has riches stored up for His body because we are "joint-heirs with Christ" (Romans 8:17). Jesus also said, "Verily, verily, I say unto you, he that believeth on me, the works that I do shall he do also; and greater works than these shall he do; because I go unto my father" (John 14:12).

In order to participate in imitating a positive change in society, we need to develop Christ-like characteristics, showing love and compassion to humanity. We must die so that God can come forth, die to our own selfish desires and ambitions. Regardless of how we feel, God is going to move. The Scriptures tell us that if the new wine is poured into old bottles or wineskins, then they will burst. The Lord told me that the new wine was about to be poured out in my life. For me to be in the center of God's perfect will, a change was necessary.

The Scriptures also tell us that God "will pour out his spirit on all flesh" (Joel 2:28). He "sendeth rain on the just and the unjust"

(Matthew 5:45). As wineskins, vessels of God, we need to be prepared for this rain, the outpouring of this new wine. The Lord told me that He was about to rain renewed anointing, fresh power, a new revelation of His Scriptures, an insight into His mind, and many other blessings in this new season. I had to go through the process of becoming a new wineskin. Regardless of how long we have been in the faith, the old mind and the old way of doing things must surely die. "The bottles break, and the wine runneth out, and the bottles perish." The wine, the blessings, the anointing, and the power will be wasted, and they will become of none effect if there is not a transformation. The blessing is that the renewed individual, containing the new thing, will be preserved.

This is God's time, and we now need to allow the Holy Spirit to have free course in the house of God. We need to allow ourselves to be used by the Lord. Unless there is a wineskin, all cannot share the wine and the wine cannot be moved from one place to another. There has to be a willingness to be the shifter of God's glory, to allow the majesty of God to be seen in our sphere of influence.

We have been called out of eternity for this hour. God desires submissive and obedient vessels. It is time for the Church to be intoxicated with what God has stored up for us. "But thou hast kept the good wine until now" (John 2:10). The good wine has been kept for you and *me*.

It is time for the Church to wake up and know who she really is, for the Bridegroom, Jesus Christ, is coming back for a prepared bride, the church. We will be known by our works or that which God has ordained for us to do. God is giving us divine governance over the earth once again. It is time for the kingdom of God to be established: firstly within us, secondly within the house of God, and thirdly within the earth.

All power is given unto us, and it is time for us to recognize it and use it. It is time for the manifestation of the "greater works," the gifts, and the ministry of the Holy Spirit. However, before we can embrace the new thing, we must first become new wineskins.

During my studies, I discovered that the Greek word *askos* means a leather bottle, wineskin, or skin. A wineskin was usually made from goatskin. The Lord immediately gave me insight concerning the process of transformation from a goatskin to a wineskin. The un-regenerated nature could not inherit the promises of the kingdom of God. The Lord then showed me the ten-step process that I would take over the course of time, which is as follows:

1. Identification – Choosing to answer the call.

2. The slaughter – Surrendering your will to the will of God concerning you.

    A. The murder – Sometimes when we surrender to the will of God, it changes the trajectory of our life, sometimes in ways that we would not desire to take.

    B. The spilling of blood – During this process, there is an exchange, receiving new life, new hopes, and new dreams.

3. The cutting away of flesh – Dealing with the lust of pursuing and satisfying our own desires.

4. Placed in a running stream – Washed by the Word of God. Our mind is renewed by the word of God. We gain a love to please God through the word.

5. Pounded with rocks – Processed by the Word of God.

6. Hung in the smoke room – Learning how to offer God pure worship.

7. The application of fresh oil – The anointing of the Holy Ghost, the commissioning, preparation and equipping for the sending forth.

8. A new covenant is established and a new identity was given.

9. Placed on the shelf to mature – Learning how to wait for the leading of the Lord.

10. A pouring out to be poured into – Daily service unto the Lord and others.

When one is going to be transformed into a vessel of honor or become effective in ministry, we often experience a change process. I had to realize that the same God that tended to the sheep was also raising the sheep for the slaughter; the very God that is protective over you will allow you to experience challenges and conflict, which will develop character. The Holman Christian Standard Bible states, "And not only that, but we also rejoice in our afflictions, because we know that affliction produces endurance, endurance produces proven character, and proven character produces hope" (Romans 5:3–4).

The sheep would one day feed others. They will become effective leaders; its flesh would be disseminated so others could live. Its skin, the covering or shell, would be a useful container for carrying the glory of God, the power of the Holy Spirit, once the sacrifice is dead. We have to become selfless to reach others. The process did not occur overnight; it took time. It was a journey over a period of five years. It was during this process that I learned to completely trust and rely on the Lord for every decision in my life. If I needed anything, it would come through the love of others. For example, when I was a single parent, my parents seemed to know when I need financial assistance or an item of clothing. I have walked out a season of no income, but my mortgage and bills were always paid, as well as every need was met. I lacked nothing. The Lord has surrounded me with so much love in action. I soon learned that we must allow God to mold us and shape us in His image and likeness. When God gets ready to send us out, we must look like Him, talk like Him, walk like Him, think like Him, and smell like Him; His heart, love, and compassion for people. We must understand the uses of the wineskin:

- Carrying water (Genesis 21:14–19) – Understanding that the principle of the word will never change, but we make the word relevant to every culture and people group.

- Storing wine (Joshua 9:4–13) – The wine is a metaphorical term, which signifies the Holy Spirit. We are required to operate the power of the spirit of God, God-conscious.

- Fermenting milk (Judges 4:19) - The fermentation process allows application of the word to all life issues.

The fermenting wine would cause the skin to stretch, and old skins would burst. I had to make a choice to either be an old wineskin or a new wineskin—to live or die. To die to self and to live in Christ would require that I go through a process of transformation, not conforming to my present world. Although this process can be difficult, we must always remember that the Lord has a wonderful plan for each believer.

The Call to the Backside of the Mountain

As I prepared myself to accept the will of the Lord, I did not realize that it was a call to the backside of the mountain. Prior to the next phase of the process, the Lord gave me a reassurance through the Scriptures. The Lord spoke into my spirit the "Living Will and Testament of the Lord Jesus Christ" for every believer:

> I have made you kings and priests unto God My Father, to whom be glory and dominion forever (Revelation 1:6). As kings and priests, you are to reign on the earth (Revelation 5:10). When you speak, say to the mountain, "Be thou removed and be thou cast into the midst of the sea," for you will have whatever you say (Mark 11:23). I desire you to know the certainty of the words of truth (Proverbs 22:21). My words are established forever in the heavens and they shall not pass away (Matthew 24:35).

> I have chosen you and not you yourselves, and ordained you that you should go and bring forth good fruit and that your fruit should remain (John 15:16). You are part of a chosen generation, a royal priesthood, a holy nation, and a peculiar people. You are required to show forth the praises of Him who has called you out of darkness into His marvelous light (1 Peter 2:9).

> Lo, I would have you to go into all the world and preach the gospel (Mark 16:15). You are My servants, whom I uphold – My elect, in whom My soul

delighteth; I have put My Spirit upon you (Isaiah 42:1). I have also put My Spirit upon you and anointed you to preach good tidings to the meek, bind up the broken-hearted, proclaim liberty to the captives, open the prison doors to them that are bound, and proclaim the acceptable year of our Lord (Isaiah 61:1–2a). I the Lord have called thee in righteousness and will hold thine hand and keep thee. You will open blind eyes, bring prisoners out of the prison, and them that sit in darkness out of the prison house. Behold, the former things are come to pass and new things do I declare: before they spring forth I tell you of them (Isaiah 42:6–9).

I want to know that the anointing which you have received of Me abideth in you, and you need not that any man teaches you: but let the same anointing teach you all things (1 John 2:27). Be sensitive to My move, listen for My voice, and look for My direction. Let your meat be to do My will and finish the work which I have started (John 4:34). For whosoever does My will is one of My brethren (Mark 3:35). For it is God which worketh in you both to will and do of His good pleasure (Philippians 2:13).

I desire My blessings to be with you. I have equipped you and empowered you; go and do My will.

I had to learn how to hold on to the Word of the Lord; I was certainly going to need it. Growing up in my home church, I felt that I was loved and protected by my Shepherd, the ministers, and the saints. I came from a strong, progressive, praying church led by a pastor with insight concerning the things of God. I learned so much from sitting at his feet and from the tutelage and guidance of other powerful men and women of God in my life. I did not realize at the time that the Lord was setting me up for survival in the wilderness, in my season of trials and difficulties. I attended nearly every Apostolic (back then it was by name and not function) Prayer Camp, every Woman of Purpose Conference, almost every Abundant Life Seminar and Training Academy, the classes presented by the International School of Biblical Studies, every WAR conference, and many other powerful conduits of the move of God in the mid to late nineties. The year 2000 was going to be a year of change.

I have learned over the course of time that so much can be accomplished when we accept God's will for our lives. The "Moses experience" means you must go alone, but God will increase you with fruit, experience, and wisdom. The daughter of Pharaoh raised Moses in a palace; I was also raised in a secure place, and God did not let me serve under the hand of a taskmaster. I knew that I was a "palace baby," rich in love and the Word. Looking back, I realized it was such a phenomenal experience. The hand of the Lord taught me, and God spoke to me, molded me, and shaped me for His purpose. God created us to be a very close-knit church family that kept our children close to our sides during the challenges of ministry. I had seen so many leaders' children become bitter against the Church and the saints because there was no balance in their homes, and I told God that I did not want to lose my children in the process of ministry. We were called into ministry as a family.

It was during this season that I learned the power of the secret place. My secret place was a place of peace, communion, and fellowship with God; I could access this anytime, anywhere. I came to the realization that the Lord was my covering, my hiding place, and my protection. It was a place that, at times, no one was privy to. Although it was a lonely place, it was a place where I came to know the Lord in a more personal way and came to know myself even more. The secret place became a place of growth and maturity. I learned that in Christ, there is a season in which isolation can lead to revelation of the things of God. There are many dimensions of God. I learned that no matter what I faced, I was privileged with the three dimensions of God experienced in the secret place:

1. Refuge – God was my shelter, my hope, and my trust. I could be completely confident, be sure, and be bold in the Lord in my journey with the Lord.

2. Fortress – God was my castle, my defense, my stronghold, and my strong place. Nothing or no one could harm me

without God's permission. Whatever I went through was designed to build me and not kill me.

3. Father – He defended me like a father. God was my supreme God, judge, and magistrate. He would legislate His promises for me in spite of the opposition of the enemy.

In the wilderness, we encounter varying types of insects and beasts, extreme heat in the day, very cold nights, and sandstorms. However, it is excellent training for developing the leader, the survivor, within us. In the wilderness, we learn what we can eat and what we cannot eat, when to hide and when it is safe to emerge, as well as what creatures are dangerous and which ones mean us no harm. We learn how to predict the weather, signal for help, and navigate our way back to a place of safety. There are so many wonderful lessons to be learned from the wilderness period, and the Lord has promised to keep His people safe through it all. In 2011, as I was coming out of the wilderness period, the Lord allowed me to share with the saints the following message from Him:

To the Saints, My Beloved Sons, and Daughters,

Upon My death, I declare that you have been "blessed with all spiritual blessings in heavenly places in Christ" (Ephesians 1:3).

1. I chose you before the foundation of the world, that you should be holy, separated, and without blame before Me in love.

2. I have predestinated you to be adopted in My lineage according to the good pleasure of My will.

3. I have made you accepted in the beloved, according to the glory of My grace.

4. You have been redeemed through My blood.

5. I have abounded toward you in all wisdom and prudence.

6. I have made known unto you the mystery of My will, according to My good pleasure, which I purposed in Myself.

7. The dispensation of the fullness of time has come, and I will now gather together in one all things in Me, Jesus Christ, both which are in heaven and which are on earth.

8. You are the praise of My glory, and I boast about you to My angels.

9. After you believed and received salvation through hearing the Word of truth, I sealed you with the Holy Spirit of promise. The Holy Spirit is the earnest of your inheritance until your redemption, My purchased possession. You will bring praise and glory to My name (Ephesians 1:4–14).

I appoint the apostles, pastors, evangelist, prophet, and teacher of My Body (the church) as executors of my will, and if they are unable or unwilling to serve, then I name the ministers as alternate executors. My executors and alternate executors shall have all powers granted by applicable laws of My kingdom to carry out all provisions of this will.

_____

Witness
Pastor Claudette Morgan-Scott, Shiloh Worship Center

Forgiveness: A Kingdom Mandate

As we are processed for ministry, we will suffer many offenses from others and even from some of the decisions we may make. Often, the offense is one of the outcomes of the learning process. Over the years, I have discovered that un-forgiveness is a disease, or what I term as a dis-ease, that is plaguing our society and is even now invading the church. Individuals in the pews, operating in the Body and sitting in the pulpit, are wounded or even maimed by this satanic stronghold. People struggle to forgive themselves and others who may have wronged them intentionally or unintentionally. The root meaning of "forgive" is to understand that someone may owe you something, perhaps morally, emotionally, or literally, but the debt is erased. Jesus lays the foundational framework for prayer, which incorporates forgiving others daily: "And forgive us our debts, as we forgive our debtors" (Matthew 6:12).

We sometimes struggle in our worship and in our day-to-day lives because we are weighed down with debts or offenses—our spiritual and moral transgressions that Jesus is unable to remove because we will not forgive others. Our level of liberty is dependent on the forgiveness and freedom we extend to others. It is essential that we do not become like the unjust servant who, though the Lord had forgiven him of all, immediately turned around and imprisoned someone else for a relatively minor debt (Matthew 18:21–35). No level of un-forgiveness is acceptable. The disciples asked how many times we should forgive our brother, and the reply was "until seventy times seven" (Matthew 18:21).

Forgiveness comes from a heart of love, compassion, and kindness toward others. The manifestations of un-forgiveness are not pretty: bitterness, anger, malice, resentment, retaliation, and the list could go on and on. We must remember "to err is human, but to forgive is divine." Forgiveness is a choice; God will not force anyone to do anything. However, for the followers of Christ, it is not an option; it is a kingdom mandate which if not followed will render you stagnant in both your walk with God and the mission that He requires of you. Some situations or injustices that you have experienced were designed to make you stronger in spiritual character and stature. Be free and move forward in your kingdom assignment! Forgiveness is extremely liberating, and it will launch you into a dimension of operation and will release supernatural blessings. Once you forgive, you are free to walk in the perfect will of God; un-forgiveness keeps you in a place of un-forgiven sins. When the Lord Jesus taught His disciples to pray, the structure for prayer included forgiveness, and the formula of forgiving others allows us to experience forgiveness from God. "And forgive us our debts, as we forgive our debtors" (Matthew 6:12). Along the journey, the Lord taught me that I need to walk in love, which is the law of Christ (Galatians 6:2). We cannot allow our roots to be bitter, for they will affect the fruit or vision that we produce.

Raising Kingdom Seeds

As a parent, I had to be cognizant of not leaving my children behind. As a child growing up, I saw so many preachers' children display resentment, bitterness, and rebellion toward their parents and the ministry. This affected me tremendously, especially as I became an adult who strived to be in the house of God. The Lord was so awesome, and He surrounded me with like-minded families who purposed in their hearts to be close to their children and still serve God. I told the Lord that if He was to call me into ministry, I did not want to lose my girls as a result of ministering to others. I soon realized that I did not have to make a choice between God and my children. My responsibility was to nurture them and teach them how to fall in love with Jesus and how to reverence Him.

As a young mother, I knew my children were an important ministry, even though I did not initially realize that we (yes, we) were called into ministry together. Some would say that I was a strict parent because I made my children listen to the Word of the Lord. Yes, they were playful children who were full of mischief, but I also recognized who they were in the Lord. I came up under a strict pastor who taught us to respect the house of God. As soon as they could write, they brought notebooks to church. They wrote down what they understood from the Word when they were only six or seven years old. I would also bring them to conferences with me. They would have their leisure time, but they would then have time to learn to hear the voice of God and respect the Word of God.

My girls and I were very close. The Lord always reminded me that they were little people, and I needed to respect them as such. They had a destiny and a future, and I was responsible for preparing them to walk in it. While the girls were very young, eight or nine years old, the Lord began to speak to me about their ministries. The Lord told me that Lertisha would walk in music ministry, be a prophetic psalmist, preach the Word of God, and offer expression through the arts. He told me that Sharna would operate in the gift of discernment, the prophetic word of knowledge, and counseling. They were both baptized in the name of the Lord Jesus Christ at the age of eight years old and soon after were filled with the Holy Ghost.

At the forefront of my mind was their destiny, and I was always trying to protect them from the hand of the enemy. It was imperative for me to be mindful of what they were exposed to and keep them covered in prayer. Both sets of grandparents were an integral part of their lives as well; they were Christians—thank you, Jesus.

It was essential to let my girls know at an early age that they had a calling on their lives, but that did not mean that they could not do extra curricular activities at school as well. As a pastor, I always had to remember that my first ministry was my family, and the girls needed to know that I would always be there for them in the triumphs and challenges of life. They did not always understand the decisions I made concerning them, but they trusted me enough to know that I loved them and cared about them, not just their callings.

The transition from England to America, the transatlantic move, was huge and did not sit well with the girls at first. It was then that the Lord told me that we would have to spend quality time together. It took time and love to walk through that process. Now, no one would know that the transition was a struggle; the love that God has developed in us for each other is so amazing.

When raising "kingdom seeds" (children), it is essential to know the gifts that God has placed inside of them. I always told my girls that they came into the earth realm on assignment and that the Lord had the assignment in mind when He sent them. We have to know the mind of God concerning our children. My girls were so different from each other, each strong-willed and stubborn in her own way. My eldest was outspoken and independent, and my youngest was a big, affectionate baby who was focused on her life goals. The Lord expressly told me not to break their will but to nurture it, for as they became immersed in the kingdom, God was going to use it. In spite of the challenges associated with transitioning from teenagers to young adults, when I look at them now, they are firm about the things of God.

It is so important that our children know that they have a special place in our hearts, one characterized by unconditional love. It's good to preach love, but our children need to see the love of God in action. They will always defend what they see. That means that our lives as pastors and church leaders need to match our lives in the home. My children had to know that they could come to their mother no matter what. Depending on the issue, they would go to the parent they felt would be most lenient. (Those kids!) I love God for allowing us the privilege of developing a strong, loving relationship, what a blessing!

We cannot force our children to walk in the destiny or calling that we see for them; we have to give them time to see it and accept it for themselves. We must remember that the fallen nature of humanity is to rebel against God. At some point in our lives, we all told God we were not able to do something. We have to be careful not to superimpose our will over their will; that becomes manipulation, which opens up the door to demonic assault. A forced assignment becomes a prison sentence; God wants our hearts not just our service. Teaching children to have a relationship with God is the best gift a parent can give them. It allows them to pursue the will of God for themselves.

I Don't Like You

During the parenting process, the phrase "I don't like you" may never be said verbally, but sometimes, our children imply it. Sometimes, the question may arise from our children: "friend or foe?" As parents, we set the parameters. There will come a season when our children will become our friends, but the role of parenting is not one that is always understood, liked, or appreciated by a child. We cannot watch our children head into a ditch and simply let them fall in. We must seek the Lord about parenting techniques and style. I have learned over the years that it is not always about winning battles, but it is about strategically planning to win the war and consistently gaining territory in our children's lives.

Our children must know that we believe in them even when they fall; their mistakes do not determine who they are. As parents, we must have great faith concerning our children, and they must hear us express that to them on a regular basis. We must let them know that we are praying for God's perfect will for their lives. There were many issues that I did not address with my children until the Lord released me to do so. Instead, I got up during the night and sought the Lord. I would anoint and pray for my children when they were asleep. I gave instructions and direction to them in the natural. The message was consistent, unwavering, and offered with love.

God-Conscious

The Lord constantly reminded me of the season of Apostle Paul's struggle:

> I find then a law, that, when I would do good, evil is present with me. For I delight in the law of God after the inward man: But I see another law in my members, warring against the law of my mind, and bringing me into captivity to the law of sin which is in my members. (Romans 7:21–23)

When raising kingdom seeds, we must remember the level of warfare that they will face because of their positioning in the kingdom. The enemy is always planning their demise and that of their parents. There are so many distractions, and we need to equip them to fight to ensure that they stay focused.

A human being consists of a spirit, a soul, and a body, and it is imperative that we teach our children's spirits to be God-conscious. The condition of the spirit will influence the condition of the soul and the manifestation displayed in the body. As parents, we have access to their heart so that that they can be sensitive to the Spirit of the Lord. We should teach them how to tap into the eternal side of their existence. I taught my girls that they came out of the eternal and that they are able to be sensitive to the Spirit of God. The Lord taught me the following:

○   The spirit is God-conscious (the breath of God).

○   The soul is self-conscious (the seat of control and wisdom).

○   The body is world-conscious (sensual consciousness: hearing, taste, touch, smell, and sight).

The Spirit of God must have ranking authority in their lives in order for them to be able to fight both the self and worldly influences. We must be Spirit-led, knowing our son-ship inheritance in Christ. We must work in unison with the Lord concerning our seeds of righteousness. It is a relationship of love and obedience, one in which we approach God in worship with a lifestyle set apart to glorify Him.

When we engage in ministry, we must not forget that family is the first ministry. The Church is comprised of families, and a correct balance in the family is essential to the health of the Church. It was important to me to be involved and often take the lead in my children's education and extra curricular activities. I was "mom" before I became a pastor, and it was important for my children to know that and feel that they were approaching their mother. After all, who wants to live with their pastor? My children did not have to make a choice between having God or other activities; they had the joy of having both.

Chapter 2
Birthing the Vision: My Story

As I began to ponder on the things that the Lord had placed in my heart, it became overwhelming to process. I knew that I would become a pastor, teach others about Christian principles and doctrine, embark on mission trips, build educational facilities, and develop communities. I started to write down my thoughts and realized that the Lord was downloading a vision. I am a firm believer that prayer (both individual and corporate) is a critical component of my spiritual walk. In prayer and times of intimacy with the Lord, there was an inception and conception of God's heart, which took place in my heart. I began to assess what was going on around me, not just in my world, but also in the world at large. My burden grew from just being concerned about my children and those that the Lord had sent to the ministry to being concerned about the future of the nation. My burden grew out of both prayer and my position as a high school administrator; I was a high school principal and a pastor at the same time for fourteen years.

I had everything I ever wanted. In the natural, there was no need for me to change my direction in life, as what I deemed important at the time was going well. I was on course for a successful career as a university professor, and I had assistance from my family in raising my children. Church was great. I attended without any responsibilities or accountability, I had no obligations, and I could hide in the background.

I began to ask myself how I could shift from just "having church" to becoming a woman of influence in my community. It was imperative that my lifestyle was one of influence for the things of God. The church is a place where God is exalted and worshipped and others are encouraged; it is also a place of power and operation of kingdom principles and mandates. I needed to be that place where God could be seen.

Well, my story is long—interesting, but long—so I will make it as brief as possible. Three years after the inception of the church, the Lord took the ministry out of the city and into a rural area between two major cities: Killeen and Belton. Each city is no more than five miles away from the church, and there are smaller developments that are closer. Some individuals wondered what we were doing, thinking the church would be too far out of town. Others fought the idea of us buying land and even decided not to relocate with us. We are currently located on the doorstep of the largest military base in the country, Fort Hood Army Base.

When we initially looked for land in 2004, we decided to purchase ten acres. We paid 25 percent down, and the landowner financed the rest of the purchase price at 8 percent for five years. In 2006, the landowner, Mr. Bob, approached us and asked us if we were still building a church. We told him yes but that we did not have any funds to do so. We were paying for the land and also for the location in the downtown area of Killeen where we were having church services. He pondered for a moment and then said he had some money that he needed to spend to reduce his tax bracket for that year and that he had always dreamt of building a church, which would be his way of giving to the Lord. We also found out that he had built homes in the past. We were so excited!

Because we were outside of the city limits, we had some latitude in making a contribution to the building project by doing some of the labor. Mr. Bob, now known affectionately as "Bob the Builder," built the church at cost price, and the church members, as well as people in the community, helped out with labor many days, evenings, and sometimes into the night. The church was completed in 2007. Mr. Bob stretched our thinking and built a two-story building when we presented him with plans for a one-story church. An apartment, which we turned into office space, was built upstairs. We were then able to finance both the land and the church with the bank and pay Mr. Bob for the land and the cost of materials to build the church. By this time, Mr. Bob, his family, and his friends became very dear friends to the ministry. He had a key to the church and would check on the facility on a regular basis.

Across the street from the church was more land: an additional ten acres. The landowner, Mr. David, approached us to let us know that he was selling the land in 2010. His price was high, and we did not have the funding to facilitate such a purchase at that time. We declined the offer. We continued in prayer, and at the end of 2011, he approached us again, reduced the price, told us we could pay whatever deposit we could afford, and said that he would owner-finance the rest of the purchase price. Wow, what a tremendous blessing! We paid 5 percent down, and he financed the remainder of the purchase price at 6 percent for seven years. That purchase was completed in March 2012. Such an amazing God! What I saw in my spirit was now starting to make sense.

It was at that point that we started the Shiloh Family Investment Group (FIG), which would make the land payments. The church was a small ministry and could not make the payments from the tithes and offerings, so twelve families got together to give a certain amount of money each month. The Lord gave us a scripture out of the book of Deuteronomy:

> For the LORD thy God bringeth thee into a good land, a land of brooks of water, of fountains and depths that spring out of valleys and hills; A land of wheat, and barley, and vines, and fig trees, and pomegranates; a land of oil olive, and honey; A land wherein thou shalt eat bread without scarceness, thou shalt not lack any thing in it; a land whose stones are iron, and out of whose hills thou mayest dig brass. (Deuteronomy 8:7–9)

When we purchased the second piece of land, my loan officer at the bank called me. He informed me that some paperwork had come across his desk and that he saw that we had purchased some land. He wanted to know what we were going to do with it. I shared with him the two projects that we had in mind: schools and homes.

I gave him a business plan for the school and the concept of the homes, which would generate income for the church and the families in the investment group. He presented the two ideas at the monthly committee at the bank. They liked the idea of the school; they felt that it would be manageable for the church and that the region needed more Christian schools. However, they also felt that we did not have the skills or knowledge to build homes. They were right—we did not, but God had a plan, and we trusted in the Lord. The vision of the Lord is always bigger than our capabilities or our resources. It can be very scary indeed and may cause us to run away or even faint. It is imperative to hear the Lord and trust in His leading.

We approached the architect that did the plans for the church to get some plans for the schools so that a builder could do an estimate for the bank. The price of the plans was way beyond our budget, and we could not move any further with the quote from the bank. We had to sit still and pray while we waited. Praying while we waited was a very difficult process; in moments like those, it's possible to wonder if God really spoke at all.

In the meantime, there were twelve acres of land behind the ten acres of land that we just purchased, and it made sense to try and get that piece also. However, we were unable to find the owner. In the early part of 2013, the Lord was dealing with us about ideas for the land and the homes we intended to build. Our goal was to pay off the land early and sow into the lives of the families at the church. Some of the saints approached an architect, only to find out that it was the architect that I had worked with on another project for my city. We met with him, and we shared our idea. He told us to try to find the owner of the twelve acres of land that we had enquired about in 2012. We found her information in the county records. It was time to be proactive and chase the dream! One of the saints and I went to her home. She was not home, but we left a message with her neighbor. She called me back the next day, and I shared with her that we would like to purchase her land. She said yes, and we were excited and began to give God glory. Again, we did not have much money, but we realized that the favor of the Lord superseded our financial situation. I learned from my spiritual father, Bishop Tudor Bismark, that favor is better than money; money is just one aspect of wealth and prosperity.

We came to an agreement, and her attorney began the paperwork. She then called and said that she had changed her mind. I began to question God again. Were we hearing correctly? We felt disappointed, but we also recognized that God was in control and that all things worked together for our good. We informed the architect of the news. He had already presented drawings based on thirty-two acres: the ten acres that the church was sitting on which we purchased from Mr. Bob, the ten acres frontage that we purchased from Mr. David, and the twelve acres that we had hoped to purchase from Ms. L. We now had to refocus, and the architect presented another set of drawings based on twenty acres.

Although we trusted God, we also began to question Him. At this point, the architect was thinking bigger than we were, and we did not have any money. We were in way over our heads, our minds, our comprehension, and our understanding. The plan went from building homes to building an entire community. We shared with him our heart for education, missions, and becoming a community resource. The Lord used the concept of building to open us up to even bigger ideas than we first anticipated.

Ms. L then contacted me and apologized for reneging on our deal. She informed me that her circumstances had changed and that she now had to sell the land. She also informed me that we could pay whatever deposit we could afford, which again was 5 percent, and she would owner-finance the remainder of the purchase price at 6 percent interest for fifteen years. This deal was much more affordable than the first offer. All three purchases were better than what a bank would have financed them for, and it amazed me that, at some point, all three pieces of land had been owner-financed.

Again, we soon realized that God was stretching us beyond our own dreams and capabilities. The plan we initially had was too small in comparison to God's plan. We felt that we were already stepping out the boat as a group of families who were not wealthy; we had simply decided to pool our resources to finance a dream. It was imperative to read the Scriptures that the Lord gave us for Shiloh FIG in order to understand what God was saying to us and the level of faith that it would take to walk this journey out. I had to understand the promises of God to the ministry and the mandate over our lives. There was a fourteen-fold promise given to us from Deuteronomy 8:7–9.

Promise	Meaning
1. A Good Land	We would walk in favor, prosperity, bountifulness, and wealth.
2. A Land of Brooks of Water	A place of inheritance which would produce seed for the sower; we would be able to fulfill the vision that the Lord had placed on our hearts in terms of missions on a local, national, and international level.
3. A Land of Fountains and Depths That Spring Out of Valleys and Hills	A fruitful place in spite of the opposition we may face from others or in our own minds
4. A Land of Wheat	Grain and productivity; we would feed others spiritually and naturally.
5. A Land of Barley	A place where fear would need to be replaced by faith.
6. A Land of Vines	The vine brings forth grapes, which produce wine. Wine is symbolic of the Holy Ghost. The Spirit of the Lord would teach us how to occupy the land by driving out previous tenants and possessing the territory that the Lord had given us. Through prayer, we would have to learn to inherit, possess, and rule our region in the realm of the spirit.

7. A Land of Fig Trees	A fig tree is a high-ranking tree, which is required to produce sweetness and good fruit. Every promised seed of Israel had a fig tree. "And Judah and Israel dwelt safely, every man under his vine and under his fig tree, from Dan even to Beersheba, all the days of Solomon" (1 Kings 4:25). What we would produce would bring us to a place of prominence and influence in the kingdom of God.
8. A Land of Pomegranates	Means to rise, exalt, get up, lift up, or mount up. Our season was now; we were shifting from a place of obscurity to a position of prominence in the natural and in the spiritual.
9. A Land of Oil Olive	The anointing of the Holy Ghost would empower us to do the work and cause the glory of the Lord to be seen in all that we would put our hands to.
10. A Land of Honey	Our project ideas would be pleasant or attractive to those that that the Lord directed us to present them to.
11. A Land Where We Will Eat Bread Without Scarceness	We would not know lack; there would be an abundance of resources available to us.
12. A Land Where We Will Not Lack Any Thing in It	We would not fall back or be brought low during this process as we stepped out in faith.
13. A Land Whose Stones Are Iron	We are lively stones, and we would be cutting edge in our thinking and project development ideas. If we stayed humble, we would be used as instruments to shape the thinking of a community and even our society; we would walk in the spirit of the pioneer.

14. A Land Out of Whose Hills We Will Dig Brass	The ideas that the Lord imparts to us would produce income and wealth for the purpose of propagating the kingdom agenda, raising a generation of God-fearing leaders, and meeting the needs of the poor.

To Be or Not to Be? That is the Question!

What do you do when everyone, including you, says it cannot be done? Often when you share your vision with people, some are excited while others are scared for you, wondering if you are in your right mind. The ministry was about to embark on one of its most difficult seasons, and it was truly a test of endurance and survival. The question then became, "Would the ministry come out of this season alive and well, or would it be broken and bitter?"

The Lord began to speak to me through concepts, and He gave me an equation:

$$\text{Vision} + \text{Voice} = \text{Purpose P (V + V)}$$

We are in the era of the resurrection of the corporate man. I heard Bishop I. V. Hilliard preach about this concept a few years ago. The church has to come together as one body, a corporate man to receive instruction for the change that is required in our region. For example in the book of Nehemiah, the people stood as one so the book of the law could be read, "And all the people gathered themselves together as one man into the street that was before the water gate; and they spake unto Ezra the scribe to bring the book of the law of Moses, which the LORD had commanded to Israel" (Nehemiah 8:1). Unity releases direction and instruction. An era is simply a period or a season marked by distinctive events or characteristics. There are events that have shaped the millennial era. For example, school shootings, the continuance of social injustice, 9/11, city and airplane bombings, the rise of propaganda through social media, the legalization of same-sex marriage, etc. We declare that this is the era.

This generation must take responsibility to be the agents of change for our society; we cannot leave the responsibility to the next generation. With the application of the kingdom blueprint, we can fulfill and maintain the kingdom agenda. We must identify, strategically pursue, and consistently maintain the kingdom agenda in our respective regions, for the church is the ruling authority in the earth realm. When the Lord gives us a vision, it is imperative what we speak over that vision, and we must be careful what voices we listen to or entertain. A voice can propel the vision forward, delay the vision, or even cause us to abort the vision. I learned over time that I had to align myself with others who had walked out a vision. For example, in 2011, I joined a network of churches called Jabula, which provides leadership training, consulting and mentoring, ministry empowerment gatherings, and ministry resource for its network of churches. The network has encouraged the churches to think about its social relevance in the community in which it is located. The social justice concern is human dignity, meeting the social needs of people in America and around the world.

Declaring and fighting for a vision that the Lord has given you is never an easy task. The vision that is transposed from heaven into our hearts and minds will tend to defy all logic and reason; our resources, means, skills, and surroundings are not usually conducive to the vision. It will often cause our minds to ponder how it will come to pass.

In any organization, you may experience opposition to developing a vision. I have heard statements like, "If it's not broke, don't fix it." Vision can be exciting and scary at the same time, and it can become contradictory as you occupy both ends of the spectrum simultaneously—the desire for change but the fear of changing. It can lead to warfare in the church, business, organization, or corporation. I call this particular illness "spiritual leukemia," a condition in which the cells turn on each other. Vision development and impartation can leave you in a vulnerable position. Given the opportunity to rule over you, will the people around you seize it or will they continue to humble themselves to the ministry that they serve in, even in the process of transition?

When Love Becomes Control

At times, the abandonment, confusion, and distress became so overwhelming for me. In pursuit of being a "good Christian," I feel that there were times when I allowed myself to be abused by others. I remember that there was a season in which I was always trying to keep the peace; I was walking in the role of middle management, attempting to please the one that I served and the ones to whom I was a servant-leader. Being a servant-leader requires you to take a stand in the dark seasons. The verbal, emotional, and psychological abuse at times became so tangible that it was suffocating. The abuse was done in the name of love, and statements like, "We're just protecting you" or "We just love you too much" were made. All of that may have been true, but I allowed myself to be controlled and manipulated, so the enemy was now ruling and reigning in that area of my life. Peter attempted to "protect" Jesus by saying that Jesus would not be crucified. Jesus strongly rebuked him, saying, "Get thee behind me, Satan." Jesus knew that He had to walk out the will of His Heavenly Fathers so that salvation would come to the world. "For God so loved the world, that he gave his only begotten Son, that whosoever believeth in him should not perish, but have everlasting life" (John 3:16). The moment we try to comply with the will of others in defiance of the will of God, we open ourselves up to the spirit of witchcraft, characterized by control and manipulation. The spirit of witchcraft causes legal demonic activity that can influence you to frustrate the plan of God concerning your life and the kingdom mandate that you came into the earth to accomplish.

Being true to the will of God is critical for every leader. There have been contentions and divisions throughout the history of the ages, between people, social groups, and nations. The scriptures declare,

> This know also, that in the last days perilous times
> shall come. For men shall be lovers of their own selves,
> covetous, boasters, proud, blasphemers, disobedi-
> ent to parents, unthankful, unholy, Without natural
> affection, trucebreakers, false accusers, incontinent,

fierce, despisers of those that are good, Traitors, heady, highminded, lovers of pleasures more than lovers of God; Having a form of godliness, but denying the power thereof: from such turn away. (2 Timothy 3:1–5)

In each season authentic leadership is incredibly difficult. A leader now faces both a war from outside of the organization (or organism, as some say) and a war from within. We expect the war from the outside, and we prepare for it; we put on our armor and gird up our minds, ready for the battle. However, we seldom prepare and are often ill-equipped for the war from within. This war is a tough one, especially if you have the spirit of the nurturer—you want the best for everyone, and you find it difficult to give up on people. Leading in this situation can be difficult if you do not also have the spirit of the father—one who will bring correction and discipline. When developing a vision, you cannot please everyone, and you cannot expect everyone to see what you see. They are located in a different spiritual position within the church or organization. You cannot get upset with others if they disagree with you; God called you to lead. A leader often has to pioneer the way from one place to another.

I have been through significant periods of vulnerability in my journey as a leader. As I began to pursue the things of God, it appeared that I also became more vulnerable and open to the assault of the enemy. I would ask the Lord, "Why am I going through this?" As a spiritual leader, I had to learn to push beyond the tears of my heart and stay focused. However, I did have to acknowledge that the tears and the brokenness were there and stop to deal with them in prayer. You cannot see clearly or walk correctly with tears in your eyes, or else, instead of hearing God, you are likely to hear yourself or someone else. The only way I achieved spiritual focus was through deep prayer and consecration, laying my all before the Lord, who knew me from my mother's womb. He knew how I felt, what I was going through, and my negative thought processes. Every day was a battle to keep my mind focused on the fact that Jesus loved me and that I existed for a purpose. The battle of the mind affected the condition of my heart, so I had to ensure that my mind was not left in a defeated state. I had to learn to see the good in others as well as the good in myself. My existence was bigger and more meaningful than I could ever have imagined.

When we go through the warfare of our minds, we must ask ourselves, "What is the enemy trying to hinder? What does he know that we don't know?" We are a priceless pearl, and you must not allow yourself to be trampled upon or misused. Our earthly existence can only be properly comprehended through a relationship with God and an understanding of our eternal existence. We existed before the foundation of the world, and we were sent into the earth realm with a specific mission in the mind of God. The Lord allowed us to come here to accomplish His will and impact the lives of others.

Operating while in pain is extremely difficult. You can get to a place where you no longer need any voices from the outside rejecting you; your inner voice is condemning you and constantly confirming your rejection. After countless situations in which I experienced rejection, I realized that it was inevitable because I was carrying that spirit around with me. I allowed it to make me miss numerous opportunities that could have been life-changing. Instead of focusing on being rejected, I began to ask myself, "How do I focus on the learning experience that life is giving me rather than the pain that comes with the experience?"

I was at the point where I felt life was unfair; I was leading while I was bleeding. I knew my life was sanctified, set apart to the Lord, but why was there so much pain, sadness, and rejection? The sense of loss on so many levels was overwhelming. I walked through years of brokenness but did not defile my garment. I operated as a single woman while in a marriage but walked upright before the Lord. Somehow, I felt that this caused me to experience even further rejection. I began to focus on the blessings of the ungodly, not understanding that the Lord rains blessings on the just and the unjust. I was not qualified to be God, and it was not my position to judge whom God should bless. We can deem ourselves to be doing the right thing, but at times, we can do it from a place of entitlement, self-righteousness, or even bitterness.

As we go through the process of being positioned, to be used of the Lord, we have to shake off every evil spirit that we entertain or that attaches itself to us; without full deliverance, a believer can be oppressed, depressed, suppressed, and obsessed. As a leader, I could not initially understand why I went through so many challenges, but after several years, I realized that the Lord was calling me to write a survival handbook for leaders who were pioneering a vision.

Unlocking Hope Deferred

> "Hope deferred maketh the heart sick: but when the desire cometh, it is a tree of life" (Proverbs 13:12).

In the process of developing a vision, we will sometimes hit road-blocks, sets backs or even experience the death of the vision. Hope deferred is simply delays in obtaining a good thing, which we passionately desire. The Hebrew word for hope is Towcheleth, meaning expectation, to wait, to be patient, be pained, stay, tarry or trust. During the period of the delay of the vision, it can be a painful experience, but we are required to wait during that season of not seeing. I had to learn to shift my mind from the Hebrew definition Towcheleth to the Greek definition Elpis, meaning, to anticipate, usually with pleasure, expectation, confidence or have faith. That was a powerful revelation. If I stayed in Towcheleth then my heart, my will, my intellect, what I understood and know would be grieved, wounded or weak. What I knew to be true, the word and promises of God would be challenged. We have to be careful that during the waiting process that we don't develop:

1. An impatient longing for a thing, a person or a place

2. A lingering dis-ease if it takes too long to come to pass

3. An uneasy mind or a skewed reality of what we know to be true

4. Despondency

5. A sinking of the spirit or heart

It is easy to become disillusioned or become delusional and start to develop another reality and give up all hope of enjoying the desired blessing or the possession of any good. We must be careful not to become hopeless or bitter during the waiting process. As I began to think about the heart being sick, I began to think about heart disease, if not taken care of it can lead to a heart attack or even death.

How you maintain during a period of sickness will determine:

a) The length of the sickness

b) Your survival rate

c) Your health when (Mind, body, and spirit) when the sickness has passed

It essential not to meditate on the blockages to the vision but to keep the blood, the life source, the word, flowing and the heart beating, even if it weak; keep pushing forward. The Lord gave me some principles through the scriptures, which are as follows:

Principles of Unlocking Hope

1. Go back to the promise – got to reaffirm in your spirit the purpose of the desire. The Lord promised Israel that the Lord would come; it's coming to pass. "Behold, I will send my messenger, and he shall prepare the way before me: and the Lord, whom ye seek, shall suddenly come to his temple, even the messenger of the covenant, whom ye delight in: behold, he shall come, saith the LORD of hosts" (Malachi 3:1).

2. Eat the book, read and digest the word of God. Let it mature and grow you.

3. You have to know the appointed time and prepare for it.

4. Stay in a posture of prayer and continue to bless God in spite of what you see. "Strengthen ye the weak hands, and confirm the feeble knees" (Isaiah 35:3).

5.   God is your strength "What is my <u>strength</u>, that I should hope? and what is mine end, that I should prolong my life?" (Job 6:11).

6.   Maintain the correct mindset. "Be of <u>good courage</u>, and he shall strengthen your heart, all ye that hope in the LORD (Psalms 31:24).

7.   Know that Lord is your guide through this process. "Behold, <u>the eye of the LORD is upon them</u> that fear him, upon them that hope in his mercy" (Psalms 33:18)

8.   Do not walk in shame because of the season of the vision. "<u>And patience, experience; and experience, hope:</u> 5 And hope maketh <u>not ashamed</u>; because the love of God is shed abroad in our hearts by the Holy Ghost which is given unto us" (Romans 5:4).

9.   Increase your faith; know and believe the word that God has spoken over you. "For we are <u>saved by hope</u>: but hope that is seen is not hope: for what a man seeth, why doth he yet hope for? But if we hope for that we see not, then do we with patience wait for it" Romans 8:24-25).

10. <u>Walk in joy and peace.</u> "<u>Rejoicing in hope</u>; patient in tribulation; continuing instant in prayer" (Romans 12:12).

Making the Invisible Visible

Before we can obtain the unseen we must focus on the unseen

- We must never look at things or circumstances
- We Must never look at physical, social or political situations
- We Must never look at our finances

We should not look to people, governments, employers, or anything or anyone else but God to meet our needs. To do so is to step outside the will of God and that will hinder the manifestation of the blessings in our life. That does not mean that the Lord cannot use people or systems to bless us, but God as our source must be the primary focus. This is what the LORD says: "Cursed is the one who trusts in man, who depends on flesh for his strength and whose heart turns away from the LORD. He will be like a bush in the wastelands; he will not see prosperity when it comes. He will dwell in the parched places of the desert, in a salt land where no one lives." [Jeremiah 17:5]

In a season where it appears that the vision has been deferred or even died, we must stay in the word of God speaking His promises to us and over the vision. The word of God is lights bringing illumination and revelation. Light reveals what has already been created in the invisible world. It is imperative to remind ourselves that we are seeking an eternal weight of glory, that Christ will be revealed and glorified in our generation (2 Cor. 4:16-18). Once we understand eternity or waiting on the Lord, we will understand more clearly time; eternity gives meaning to time. The waiting period often brings affliction as you begin to doubt or those around you begin to doubt the voice of God. Affliction makes us desire the glory, remember, the greater the affliction, believe, the greater the glory. Hope is the interval between the promise of God and its fulfillment.

A Tree of Life

The scripture declares that when the desire comes to pass it will become a tree of life. We must know what we are carrying or getting ready to produce. I was encouraged to know that:

1. The Lord wants our desires to come to pass; He puts them in our hearts

2. A good desire is being a tree of life or to become a tree of life

3. We must become a desire of all nations and to bless all nations – bring redemption to all who we encounter

4. But when the desire cometh — When the good desired and the expected is obtained it is a tree of life like the Garden of Eden — That is, most sweet, satisfactory, and

reviving to the soul, it gives all those who partake of or encounter the vision unspeakable pleasure and delight.

The following scriptures become a critical component of knowing the heart of God; the nation needs healing and solutions now:

1. Proverbs 11:30 - The fruit of the righteous *is* a tree of life; and he that winneth souls *is* wise.

2. Proverbs 3:18 - She *is* a tree of life to them that lay hold upon her: and happy *is every one* that retaineth her.

3. Revelation 22:2 - In the midst of the street of it, and on either side of the river, was there the tree of life, which bare twelve manner of fruits, and yielded her fruit every month: and the leaves of the tree were for the healing of the nations.

Chapter 3

Imparting the Vision

At this point in the journey, we as a church had to put our faith into action and commit to believing the Word of the true and living God who has all things in His hands. With God, nothing is impossible. The Lord gave us a clear mission and a strategic plan for our ministry:

Ten-Phase Project

1. Christian life family center: classrooms, counseling center, and mission's office
2. Housing development on plot Shiloh-3: homes, walking trail, and dog park
3. Commercial offices on plot Shiloh-1
4. Ancillary services: concierge service and community center
5. Elementary school
6. Day care
7. Middle school
8. Science park
9. Commercial offices and entertainment center
10. High school

The vision is not corporately developed; it is corporately caught and then taught (Bishop Tudor Bismark).

When I first heard this quote, it became a turning point in my mind-set. My expectations of others changed as God began to develop the vision in the ministry. I realized that God gives the vision to a set man or woman, and the assignment of those around the visionary is to help clarify and unfold that vision. It is the vision of God, not the vision of man, and it is imperative to ensure that no one is allowed to add to or take away from that vision. This means that the visionary needs to spend time with the Lord to ensure that they have heard a clear word. The visionary must also check the motives of those around him or her and consider how they might benefit from the vision or how the vision might challenge them or make them uncomfortable. The vision of the Lord is given to forge a process of change in an individual, a ministry, a community, a region, or even a nation.

The development of a vision can be a very uncomfortable process. In many ways, it is similar to a pregnancy. In a marriage, when a woman is intimate with her spouse, pregnancy is often likely, anticipated, welcomed, and exciting. Often, we cannot wait to announce the pregnancy to others, but soon after, the reality sets in regarding the longevity of the task ahead and the arduous nature of carrying a baby (or babies) for nine months. The shock begins to set in with morning sickness, swelling, stretch marks, and other unwelcome symptoms.

The Lord took me to Numbers 21 to show me what we had to face and how to be strategic along the journey. I noticed that the Lord gave the promises before the process. If I had known the process first, I would not have even wanted to hear the promise, and I would not have attempted the rough terrain of the journey! The Lord showed me a "21-Step Journey" in Numbers 21:10–35 where the children of Israel encountered places or people, which begins "And the children of Israel set forward." I call it "The 21/21 Journey," 21 steps from Numbers 21. The word of God is phenomenal; God was showing me who and what I could encounter when birthing a vision, not literal places or people, but possible hindrances. He directed me to look up the Hebrew meaning of every city that the Israelites journeyed through and the people they encountered in that chapter, the details of which can be found in appendix 1. I learnt that we should not be surprised by the possible obstacles, as the Israelites made it to the land of promise in spite of the obstacles they encountered along the journey.

The first occurrence of the word "vision" in the Word can be found in Genesis chapter 15: "After these things the word of the LORD came unto Abram in a vision, saying, Fear not, Abram: I am thy shield, and thy exceeding great reward" (Genesis 15:1). The Hebrew word used for vision in this verse is *machazeh*. "Vision" means to perceive or to contemplate with pleasure. Specifically, to have a vision means to behold, look, prophesy, provide, or see. A vision is the visual confirmation of the audible voice of God.

Often, a vision is associated with fear and risk-taking; it is seldom associated with rewards without a sacrifice. It was necessary for the Lord to encourage Abram. When God speaks, we need to ensure that we move with clarity and confidence; Abram had to take a journey with a clear indication of the full extent of what his future would hold. The Lord told Abram three specific things:

- Fear not – instilling confidence
- I am thy shield – bringing protection
- I am thy exceeding great reward – providing unlimited benefits

Another excellent example is Moses. In the process of developing the vision, there were times and seasons in which Moses had to step back, go to the mountain, and receive instruction and direction. Despite all of the wisdom of Jethro, his father-in-law, Moses was still the one who was called. Moses could not take Jethro to the mountain with him—not even to the foot of the mountain, which was Joshua's assignment. Moses went to the top of the mountain, and Joshua, the warrior, guarded the foot of the mountain to ensure that Moses did not experience any interruptions during the download. The Lord knew that it would take the spirit and heart of Joshua to fulfill the vision that God had given to Moses for His beloved people Israel. God had a specific plan that would release blessings for His people and keep His continual covering over the chosen nation.

As the visionary, you need to remember that the Lord has made you responsible for the vision. Shifts can be difficult, especially when people have supported you loyally over a number of years, but it is necessary to discern when their assignments have changed. You have to maintain a spirit of discernment, as well as a clear focus. After the necessary shifts have been made, the people God has selected to be around you can help you determine how the vision should unfold. Their wise counsel will aid in developing strategies to make things happen. Their roles have to be clearly defined in order to support, promote, and fulfill the God-given vision; their collective assignment is never to change the vision but to help in the unfolding of the vision.

As previously mentioned, the reality of the long, arduous nature of carrying a vision eventually sets in for the visionary. During the process, the visionary and those around him or her can sometimes become very uncomfortable. The vision of the Lord will change your present reality and disturb your comfort zone. As leaders, God will often create a hunger in our hearts to address the spiritual, social, and economics needs of society. The closer we get to the Lord Jesus Christ, the more we come to the realization that we cannot continue to have church as usual and ignore the plight of those who are groaning and waiting for the manifestation of the sons of God; they are waiting for us, the Church, the remnant, the kingdom builders.

During this time, the Lord began to stir up the spirit of the pioneer in me. It was in this season that I learned how to endure hardship like a good soldier—to keep moving forward toward my dreams and goals no matter the adversity or opposition. There were times when I felt that God was asking too much and that the personal scarifies and losses were too great, but I learned early in the journey to count the cost and pay the price. There is no better place to be than in the will of God. I could no longer sit back and make someone else responsible for changing my immediate world.

In the process of vision development, people around you may see a noticeable change in your focus. This may cause some insecurity in those individuals that are used to seeing you operate in a particular way or experience a lack of attention on their individual needs due to a change of focus toward the vision. I have learned over time that the relationships that leaders may experience may suffer enormous challenges from outside forces and internal struggles. Every time we experience change, it upsets the equilibrium of our relationships with others and constant readjustment is required; this takes a concerted effort by both parties concerned.

The Lexium Experience

As I began to meditate upon vision, I fell into a deep sleep in November 2016; when I worked up, I heard the word *Lexium*, a term that I had never heard before. The Icelandic Online Dictionary and Readings define the term *Lexium* as "lessons learned" or "experience" (2016). As a pioneer, you have to learn to deal with your disappointments and failures as well as your successes and use every experience as a learning experience. Sometimes what we may determine as a failure is actually a route diversion that the Lord can use for your good. The scriptures declare, "And we know that all things work together for good to them that love God, to them who are the called according to his purpose" (Romans 8:28). As a child of God, we must be cognizant of the fact, the eternal God knew we would experience failures, but He also knew that we would rise above them, bringing Him glory and honor in all things. We cannot stay in a place where we lick our wounds, but we must allow the Lord to bind them up and move forward. Romans 8:29–30 provides a four-step process of the Christian journey:

We were predestined, ordained to walk the path that was set before us; we have a choice to walk in that path. Rank and order were bestowed upon us, moving us from a place of obscurity to the fore-front; we were called. In spite of our human failings, we have made righteous or we are in right standing with God, because of who He is not and not because of anything we have done. To be glorified means to be esteemed with honor and majesty, what a privilege to serve the kingdom of God. The Lord has been extremely gracious toward us. Failures do not automatically determine incompetency, but rather, we must use it as a learning experience.

The apostle Paul told the Roman church,

> And not only so, but we glory in tribulations also: knowing that tribulation worketh patience; And patience, experience; and experience, hope: And hope maketh not ashamed; because the love of God is shed abroad in our hearts by the Holy Ghost which is given unto us. (Romans 5:3–5.

Even in the secular world, we are approved by our experiences. That is why resumés and curriculum vitae are essential components of job selection, as well as interviews, which determine the character and your ability to relate your experience to real-life scenarios. Some of the most successful people had some of the greatest disappointments or failures. The world-renowned cinematic entrepreneur, Steven Spielberg was rejected from the University Southern California's School of Cinematic Arts on two occasions before his success. His teachers told Thomas Edison, the one acclaimed for creating the light bulb, that he was "too stupid to learn anything." Edison went on to hold more than one thousand patents, including the phonograph and practical electric lamp. Albert Einstein shaped the world know in terms of physics; although, he did not start speaking until the age of four years old, and the list could go on and on. We should be apt to learn from every experience; we have been qualified by the Lord Jesus Christ to undertaken any and every given assignment. As leaders, we must identify the lessons gained along the journey and be willing to teach others. Learning is an on-going process; we may not like the process of learning, but the rewards are extremely empowering. God is so amazing; He has a way of causing us to arise from a place of doubt and insecurity to a place of victory. Gideon doubted that God was with him, "And Gideon said unto him, Oh my Lord, if the LORD be with us, why then is all this befallen us? and where be all his miracles which our fathers told us of, saying, Did not the LORD bring us up from Egypt? but now the LORD hath forsaken us, and delivered us into the hands of the Midianites" (Judges 6:13). Gideon learned how to believe God, trust God, and obey God. Lessons are extremely imperative. Gideon's army was reduced from thirty-two thousand to three hundred. The Lord told Gideon, "And the LORD said unto Gideon, By the three hundred men that lapped will I save you, and deliver the Midianites into thine hand: and let all the other people go every man unto his place" (Judges 7:7). We must be confident going forward in the things of God.

The Road to Success

I began to think generationally in 2011–2012. I realized that I had to develop a plan that lasted beyond my generation or that of my children; I had to leave a legacy in the community that would bless the generations to come. One example was the development of a Christian school that would raise leaders who would develop policies for various organizations and develop mind-molders in education that would be Christ-centered. We needed to raise children to be Christian leaders that would raise Christian leaders, etc. If we influenced a generation, they could influence the next generation and ensure that we push forward a biblical worldview. Another example was creating buildings and resource centers that would become a vital component of community resources. This way of thinking was affirmed when I attended my first Jabula Conference in Detroit in the spring of 2012, under the leadership of Bishop Tudor Bismark and Bishop Hugh Daniel Smith. I realized that I needed to surround myself with people of faith who thought beyond their generation. When Moses sent the spies into the land of promise, he had to decide whose report he would believe: the report of the optimistic minority or that of the pessimistic majority. Perhaps that sounds like a simple choice, but it can be very difficult when the majority has the loudest voice. I had to learn to tune those pessimistic voices out and listen to the voice of the Lord. The ten spies, the majority, had valid reasons why the children of Israel should not go forward. However, that stance required no faith whatsoever; it was a report based on what was and not on what could be, with the Lord on their side. It was imperative for me to develop the mind-set of the risk-taker, along with a "take over" attitude. For example, although I heard the Lord say that I would build a church, I only had enough money to put a deposit down on some land and pay rent in our current facility. I certainly did not have any money to build. I had to trust that the Lord was in control of each step even if I could not see the entire outcome; I had to be obedient at each step of instructions. The Lord is not setting us up for failure. His desire is for us to succeed in all assignments and bring Him glory. I had to be encouraged in the Lord through the words that the Lord gave to Joshua after Moses died:

> There shall not any man be able to stand before thee all the days of thy life: as I was with Moses, so I will be with thee: I will not fail thee, nor forsake thee. Be strong and of a good courage: for unto this people shalt thou divide for an inheritance the land, which I sware unto their fathers to give them. Only be thou strong and very courageous, that thou mayest observe to do according to all the law, which Moses my servant commanded thee: turn not from it to the right hand or to the left, that thou mayest prosper whithersoever thou goest. (Joshua 1:5–7)

I had to decide in my heart whether to be an agent of change or to be changed by the society in which I lived. Values and ideologies are forever changing, and I felt they were not changing for the better; Christian values were being compromised daily and even been ridiculed as old-fashioned or politically incorrect. As a pioneer, it was essential to develop a relentless attitude as a warrior; to gain territory, demonic spirits must be driven out and new spiritual thrones established. I made up my mind that positive change was non-negotiable; it was absolutely necessary if I was to pass on a righteous legacy to the next generation. The church must have a "single eye" and a strong biblical worldview.

> The light of the body is the eye: therefore when thine eye is single, thy whole body also is full of light; but

when thine eye is evil, thy body also is full of darkness. (Luke 11:34)

Proper Perspective – What we doing is to always glorify God and help
others. I have a responsibility to point people to Christ. When we are
focused on the principles and the doctrines of Christ, we can do so;
we are the light of the world that carries truth. Jesus is still the answer
to healing a confused, dying world. We cannot be ashamed to profess
our faith in the Lord Jesus Christ.

Accurate Vision – Once we walk as children of the light, we will be
able to see clearly, seeing the things that God sees, providing the solution to social, political, economic, and other problems that we face
locally, nationally, and sometimes even globally.

Righteous Judgment – God is a God of righteousness and judgment.
The Holman Christian Standard Bible using the word *justice*, meaning judgment, "He loves righteousness and justice; the earth is full of
the LORD's unfailing love" (Psalms 33:5). God is concerned about
both in our society, righteous laws that ensure justice, to include
social justice for all people.

The Lord spoke to me and said that He needed some "yes men"
and "yes women" who would not question Him but instead would
speak life over the vision; this is about ultimately saying yes to the
Lord, not expecting everyone around you being a yes person. This
process may take time while we have people in our lives that can
critique us, challenge us, and help us to see our blind spots in vision
development and implementation.

- ○ We speak life in the name of Jesus!
- ○ God can do it!
- ○ It is God's will!
- ○ Now is the appointed time!
- ○ The favor of God is on the vision!
- ○ We declare and decree that the Lord Jesus will do it!

It is imperative that we understand the concept of vision if we are to become an effective force that is advancing the kingdom of God in the earth realm. The Hebrew word for vision is *machazeh*, which comes from the word *chazah*. Vision is accomplished mentally. Vision also means to perceive or contemplate (with pleasure). According to the Hebrew definition of the word "vision," one must have the ability to behold or to see something that is not yet seen, believing that the unknown can become known and the invisible can become visible. The Hebrew definition of vision also indicates that with vision comes prophecy. You have to be able to speak that which you see in the supernatural in order to bring it to the natural realm.

God often makes things known in visions. The purpose of a vision is to establish in the earth realm what is already established in the realm of the spirit: the will and the kingdom of God.

> And he said, Hear now my words: If there be a prophet among you, I the LORD will make myself known unto him in a vision, and will speak unto him in a dream. (Numbers 12:6)

God gives us visions so that we will not fear that which He has commissioned us to accomplish. We need to know our eternal Father as the great I Am. God introduces Himself in this way in order to establish that there is no failure in Him. In the process of speaking to Moses, the Lord made it known that He was Abram's shield and exceeding great reward, indicating that Abram may face some challenges but that it was necessary for Abram to remember who spoke to him, who commissioned him, and who would send provision for the vision to come to pass. The Lord called Abram into a place that was unfamiliar to him:

> And Terah took Abram his son, and Lot the son of Haran his son's son, and Sarai his daughter in law, his son Abram's wife; and they went forth with them from Ur of the Chaldees, to go into the land of Canaan; and they came unto Haran, and dwelt there. (Genesis 11:31)

The land of Ur was located in the east, a region of light or fire, in the land of the Chaldees, according to the *Strong's Exhaustive Concordance of the Bible* reference 03778, Chaldees was a place of astrology. Abraham (Abram) was sent to the land of Canaan or the place of humiliation and trafficking (The *Strong's Exhaustive Concordance of the Bible* reference 03667); he was moving from a place of comfort to a place of challenge.

A vision will often change our current position or spiritually, physically, or psychologically perspective. A kingdom vision is propelled by a kingdom mandate, which supersedes our ability to achieve what we see. We must remember that the vision is for an appointed time, and we have to access the window of opportunity at the appointed time. The vision must be executed on time (not too early) and in time (not too late). We must remember that what God sends out of the spiritual realm is eternal, located in *kairos* time (a moment in time when something happens); we must be able to place the vision in *chronos* time, or chronological time, when it is entrusted to us. I believe that the season of casting visions is currently upon us for the following reasons:

- Jesus is trying to *reveal* to us the riches of His Father's—to take the cover off, disclose, place in time the father's presence in our communities and the United States.

- Like no other time that I have experienced, it is the season of miracles; events in the natural world brought about by God that cannot be discerned by the senses, but are orchestrated by divine activity; we need a healing for our nation.

- We need a demonstration of power that interrupts the laws of nature and man—a supernatural move of God, an interference with the ordinary.

- We need people sealed with a divine mission to be released on assignment.

When God speaks to you, it is specifically to fulfill His will; it is good, acceptable, and perfect. Roman 12:2 states the following:

> And be not conformed to this world: but be ye transformed by the renewing of your mind, that ye may prove what is that good, and acceptable, and perfect, will of God.

The New Era

As we enter into a new political era, with the election of a new president and a new political party in the United States, there is a change in the spiritual climate in the American church. I have come to realize that the process is not an easy one. There are differing views as to the role of the Church in today's changing society. In shifting the focus of the church from simply gathering for weekly services to occupying kingdom or societal assignments, I too faced some challenges. Earlier, I called the internal warfare of the body "spiritual leukemia," a sickness in which the cells turn on each other. What we deem as integral components of the Church can sometimes be fighting among them.

There may be times when you begin to ask the Lord why you are located in a particular place at a particular time going through certain experiences. You will have to seek the face of God for an answer. There are times as a leader when what you go through seems to make no sense and you begin to feel that you should not have to deal with this, but you will come to realize that there really is purpose in everything. You cannot move out of a particular battle if the Lord has determined that you need to learn something.

In this new season, we must catch the vision and prepare for the transition; there has to be a paradigm shift. Paradigms belong to the realm of concept, and then they birth structure. We have to cause the Church to move from one place to another, altering the systematic operation of business as usual. We have to be in alignment with heaven and with the vision that God has for each center or house of worship.

The era has changed from the Gospel of salvation from sin to the Gospel of the kingdom. What exactly does this mean?

- *The Gospel of Salvation from Sin* – The "gospel of salvation" primarily addresses the good news that God, through Christ's death and resurrection, has provided a means of salvation from sin.

- *The Gospel of the Kingdom* – The "gospel of the kingdom" is a more complete gospel, which not only addresses God's provision for salvation from sin but also His provision for taking dominion in every system of society.

We are going back to the original plan of God, the Eden mandate: "And God blessed them, and God said unto them, be fruitful, and multiply, and replenish the earth, and subdue it: and have dominion over the fish of the sea, and over the fowl of the air, and over every living thing that moveth upon the earth" (Genesis 1:28). In our time, God has revealed a new strategy for taking this dominion; the strategy is called the "Seven-Mountain Mandate." The way to take dominion is to take control of the seven most influential societal institutions called "mountains." It is imperative to have a clear knowledge base and understand of the societal systems and how they interact with each other; sometimes education, experience, or by divine appointment is a key that will allow access to these systems. These mountains include the following:

- government
- media
- family
- business and finance
- education
- church and religion
- arts and entertainment

Deborah was a prophetess recorded in the Old Testament book of Judges 4. She was the only female judge, a judicial leader, to the Jewish people. Her primary role was to judge Israel, leading to the arbitration of a just and righteous resolution. Deborah had divine knowledge from the Lord and was sort out when military leaders went to war. Like Deborah, we have been anointed to lead during this season—to speak, subdue, commune, command, declare, destroy, and teach. We are now required to be generational thinkers, and we must ask, "How can I impact the next five generations, the next one hundred years?" It is the hour of emergence for the Church, catalyzed by a recognition that the kingdom of God that is within us must be manifested in all areas of society. We must make an impact and leave a righteous legacy for the generations to come. It is the time and the season for the church to take back and maintain the divine ordering of the affairs of the world through our visibility in all of the major public arenas.

We have an appointment with destiny and purpose, and the favor of the Lord is upon us as we walk out the perfect will of God during this season. What is your divine appointment? In this dispensation, there is a divinely appointed order that has been legislated in the heavens, and this is the greatest hour of the Church—you and me.

As I began to meditate upon the depth and complexity of "casting the vision" of the Lord, He began to deposit some things in my spirit that encouraged and excited me:

o   God is going to move regardless of any obstacles or opposition, simply because He is God and He reigns; we may cause blockages to His move, but we will not hinder that move.

o   The grace of God is on our lives to fulfill our divine purpose in the perfect will of God.

o   God is redeeming the time and taking us back to the original plan.

o   We have to know each other's anointing and measure of rule to effectively execute the vision.

o   God reminded me of something I heard Bishop Tudor Bismark and other preachers state, "We need Daniels to deal with the political issues and Ezekiels to deal with the church folks."

o   We need to ask for a move of God, and not force a move of God; we must seek clear direction through prayer.

o   We need a real move of the Holy Spirit; self has to get out of the way!

o   The move of God has to be holy, and it has to manifest the power of God throughout the whole world! We need the weight of the manifested glory of God in the earth realm. God is still God, and beside Him, there is no other!

Chapter 4

Vision Blockers

As I began to study vision, the Lord began to deal with me about vision blockers. My definition of the term *vision blockers* 'denotes an individual, system, or process that may temporarily hinder or delay the implementation of a kingdom or corporate vision'. The concept will be explored further in this chapter with the examination of the lives of Lot, the nephew of Abraham; Eli, a priest in Israel who raised the prophet Samuel and Uzziah, king of Israel during the time of the Prophet Isaiah; and finally Jezebel, the Phoenician princess who married King Ahab during the time of Elijah the prophet. These were the spirits I encountered during the vision development process, and it was helpful for me to be able to identify them; it allowed me to be focused when praying for the vision. Please remember, "For the weapons of our warfare are not carnal, but mighty through God to the pulling down of strong holds" (2 Corinthians 10:4). I am sure there are others spirits that other visionaries may have experienced. What I have learned is to locate them in the scriptures so you know how to pray against them.

The Lotian Spirit

As I studied the life of Lot, the nephew of Abraham, I coined the term "The Lotian Spirit," describing his character and behavior. The Scriptures declare in Genesis 11:31, "And Terah took Abram his son, and Lot the son of Haran his son's son, and Sarai his daughter in law, his son Abram's wife; and they went forth with them from Ur of the

Chaldees, to go into the land of Canaan; and they came unto Haran, and dwelt there."

Lot was chosen to walk with his uncle to find a city whose builder and maker was the Lord. In this chapter, *Abram* and *Abraham* refers to the same person; Abraham's name change can be found in Genesis 17:5 as God declared that he would move from being a father to a father of many nations. Uncle Abraham, sometimes called Father Abraham, was in pursuit of the promises of God and took his nephew with him. One might have thought that because Lot was provided with such an incredible opportunity that he would have allowed himself to be mentored by his uncle and walk in the generational promise. Many times, however, the people that we bring with us on our journey do not have the heart that is required to ensure the fulfillment of the vision. We must ensure that those who choose to walk out the journey with us, family included, do not change the course of the journey, the destination of the journey, or delay the arrival to the set destination.

Lot eventually took his stuff and parted ways with his uncle, but he did not realize that his blessings were based on connection and proximity to the one whom God had chosen. As we read Genesis 13, we see the dispute between Abraham and Lot play itself out:

> And Abram said unto Lot, Let there be no strife, I pray
> thee, between me and thee, and between my herd-
> men and thy herdmen; for we be brethren. Is not the
> whole land before thee? separate thyself, I pray thee,
> from me: if thou wilt take the left hand, then I will go
> to the right; or if thou depart to the right hand, then
> I will go to the left. And Lot lifted up his eyes, and
> beheld all the plain of Jordan, that it was well watered
> every where, before the LORD destroyed Sodom and
> Gomorrah, even as the garden of the LORD, like the
> land of Egypt, as thou comest unto Zoar. Then Lot
> chose him all the plain of Jordan; and Lot journeyed
> east: and they separated themselves the one from the
> other. Abram dwelled in the land of Canaan, and Lot
> dwelled in the cities of the plain, and pitched his tent
> toward Sodom. (Genesis 13:8–12)

Abraham was rich in cattle, gold, and silver. The Scriptures declare that the land could provide resources for both Abraham's and Lot's cattle and herdsmen. They started the journeyed together, but due to some disagreements between the herdsmen, a separation became necessary. As a leader, you will begin to sense in your spirit when a conflict in vision is looming. I now know that it is better to allow people to leave than to hinder the vision.

When deciding how to divide the land, Abraham's perception was spiritual while Lot's perception was natural. Lot looked at the immediate gratification of the richness of the land and pursued what he felt was the more strategic plan. However, Lot did not realize that what appeared to be flourishing was about to be destroyed and brought low. The Word of God tells us that "Lot went up out of Zoar, and dwelt in the mountain, and his two daughters with him; for he feared to dwell in Zoar: and he dwelt in a cave, he and his two daughters" (Genesis 19:30).

According to the *Strong's Exhaustive Concordance of the Bible* reference 06820, *Zoar* means a little or to be small—a place that is ignoble or to be brought low. Lot ended up losing everything: he was made bare and naked and the daughter that he produced positioned him to be sexually exploited by, the misuse of his reproductive seed. I refuse to believe that the Lord delivered Lot from the hand of the enemy only to be raped by his daughters. God's intent was for Lot to be delivered from a place where God was not honored and realign him and his family the generational blessings of his uncle. Instead, Lot reproduced seed out of the divine order of God.

Everyone may not see, understand or agree with your vision; endure the course, and pursue the long-term blessing. We must be careful not to produce anything or allow those around us to produce anything outside of the will of God or produce a substitute of the vision. Lot went for the greener pasture but in the end produced an illegal seed, the Moabites, which were an enemy to the promised seed of God. Every birth or area of production may not be legitimate; it may not be in accordance with established rules, principles, or standards that God has set for the body of Christ.

What one produces outside of the perfect will of God is illegitimate and brings the Lord no glory. "An Ammonite or Moabite shall not enter into the congregation of the LORD; even to their tenth generation shall they not enter into the congregation of the LORD for ever" (Deuteronomy 23:3). We cannot continue to ask God to bless what He did not father.

Out of Lot's experience and the incestuous birth of his son and grandson came forth death, deception, grief, self-hate, abandonment, rejection, denial, outrage, painful and potentially problematic clinical dilemmas and challenges, rebellion, disobedience, lack of wisdom, guilt, shame, and illegitimacy. That seed hated the seed of the promise. "And he said unto them, follow after me: for the LORD hath delivered your enemies the Moabites into your hand. And they went down after him, and took the fords of Jordan toward Moab, and suffered not a man to pass over" (Judges 3:28). Every negative seed, thought, word, or belief system needs to be cut off at the root so that the promised seed of God can reign in the earth realm. The story of Abraham and Lot demonstrates that you have to be careful who accompanies you on your journey. Even if you don't see the promise at the beginning of the journey believe the word of God.

Instead of repenting and returning to his uncle's house, his covering, Lot went back to a familiar way of worship as we see in 1 Kings 11:33; we see that the Moabites worshiped Chemosh and did not do what was right in eyes of the Lord. Lot or his daughters must have taught this way of life; the Moabites sphere of influence. The Hebrew definition for Chemosh is "to subdue the powerful." There was a constant struggle between the Israelites and the Moabites, a struggle that metaphorically represented the following dualities:

1. the promise and the lie
2. faith and fear
3. confidence and arrogance
4. the legitimate and the illegitimate

The vision that the Lord imparts into the earth realm is powerful and will change nations and the course of history. When confronted with the release of the Moabitish spirit, you must respond like Jehoshaphat in 2 Chronicles 20—you must worship and praise God. Your enemies will end up destroying themselves, and "you have no need to fight in this battle" (2 Chronicles 20:17). Stay focused and stay the course!

The Elian Spirit

The books of Samuel are some of my favorite books in the Bible, not just because the scripture for our church comes from one of those books, but because they are full of so much fascinating history. In the beginning of the first book of Samuel, Eli was the priest of the temple and was responsible for ensuring that proper worship was offered to the Almighty God.

However, what was disturbing about Eli was his inability to recognize the groaning of the earth for a move of God. In 1 Samuel 1:10, it declares that Hannah was in bitterness of soul and wept, seeking the face of God for a new life. Her husband favored her over his other wife, but she was unable to produce a child for her husband. Eli did not understand that although the Lord favors the Church, productivity is still necessary. I see Hannah as a metaphor for the Church, and her rival Peninnah was producing seed and taunting her.

The United States is facing crisis after crisis, and the *Daily News* recently reported that "God isn't fixing this" (December 2, 2015) after fourteen people were killed in a California mass shooting. God is being blamed for the ills of the world and the corrupt hearts of mankind, but the Church must continue to seek the Lord for a seed that will bring change, a solution, and a vision in spite of the mocking. Eli failed to interpret the needs of his time:

> And it came to pass, as she continued praying before
> the LORD, that Eli marked her mouth. Now Hannah,
> she spake in her heart; only her lips moved, but her
> voice was not heard: therefore Eli thought she had been
> drunken. And Eli said unto her, How long wilt thou be

drunken? put away thy wine from thee. And Hannah answered and said, No, my lord, I am a woman of a sorrowful spirit: I have drunk neither wine nor strong drink, but have poured out my soul before the LORD. Count not thine handmaid for a daughter of Belial: for out of the abundance of my complaint and grief have I spoken hitherto. (1 Samuel 1:12–16)

The Church needs the righteous leaders to conceive effective ideas, visions, or ministries, and the seeds that are produced will bless the body as well as the community; everyone benefits from the vision of the Lord. As God's leaders and guardians over change, we must be careful not to operate in our gifts alone without the anointing. Eli's name means "lofty." We must connect to the mind and heart of God and not be lifted up above the Lord. All leaders require a relationship with the Lord through intercession and worship. Eli knew when the Lord was speaking to Samuel, but Eli no longer heard the voice of the Lord for himself. Eli was too far from God to hear him.

Eli's sons violated the temple with fornication and evil dealings. Despite being both their priest and their father, Eli failed to correct his sons, and in light of this, I have coined the term "the Elian spirit." The Elian spirit will recognize the hindrances to the move of God but will not make the necessary changes to align the people or the Church to see or hear God. The immediate need to please others will always take precedence. Eli's sons recognized that there was power in the Ark of the Covenant, the presence of the Lord; however, they tried to bring the glory into the wrong battle through an illegal move. Eli's sons took the Ark of the Covenant, which contained a pot of manner, the rod of Aaron and the Ten Commandments, into battle with the philistines. The Ark of the Covenant signified the presence, the promise, and the glory of God. "And the ark of God was taken; and the two sons of Eli, Hophni and Phinehas, were slain" (1Samel 4:11). Thirty thousand soldiers from the camp of the Israelites were killed. When you refuse to follow the Lord's instructions or we move in fear or disobedience, we may experience some opposition emotionally, psychologically, or spiritually. The scriptures said that when Eli heard that the ark was taken, "And it came to pass, when he made mention of the ark of

DR. CLAUDETTE MORGAN-SCOTT

God, that he fell from off the seat backward by the side of the gate, and his neck brake, and he died: for he was an old man, and heavy. And he had judged Israel forty years" (1 Samuel 4:18).

The Uzziahian Spirit

The Lord took me to the book of Isaiah, and He began to talk to me about king Uzziah, also known as Azariah. He was a king of the ancient kingdom of Judah and one of Amaziah's sons. Uzziah was sixteen when he became king of Judah, and he reigned for fifty-two years. The first twenty-four years of his reign were as coregent with his father, Amaziah. I also coined the phrase "The Uzziahian Spirit."

The Scriptures indicate that the prophet Isaiah had a vision during a time when the children of Israel were in sin: "The vision of Isaiah the son of Amoz, which he saw concerning Judah and Jerusalem in the days of Uzziah, Jotham, Ahaz, and Hezekiah, kings of Judah" (Isaiah 1:1). The vision was one of judgment and destruction. However, what Isaiah was able to see changed when the ranking authority in the region changed: "In the year that king Uzziah died I saw also the Lord sitting upon a throne, high and lifted up, and his train filled the temple" (Isaiah 6:1). What you see is determined by what is alive in your life or in your atmosphere.

It is important for us to know who Uzziah is in this passage. His name means the "strength of Jah, the Lord most vehement." His father was King Amaziah, whose name also means "strength of Jah," and his mother was Jecoliah, or "Jah will enable." Uzziah had a spiritual DNA that was undergirded by the strength of the Lord, and he could access that power if he allowed himself to tap into the anointing or covering over the lives of his parents. However, his lineage was not perfect. Although his grandfather Joash did what was right in the sight of God and restored proper worship in Judah, he failed to deal with the ancestral curses of his grandmother Athaliah and his great-grandparents Ahab and Jezebel. There was also a tendency in his lineage to steal the glory of the true and living God and worship other gods instead (2 Chronicles 24:11–12).

After the death of Uzziah's grandfather Joash, his father Amaziah began to reign. He did what was right in the sight of the Lord but with an impure heart. His motives were wrong. Developing a vision requires us to check our own hearts to ensure that we are doing the will of the Lord for the right reasons; there can be no room for self-glory. In 2 Chronicles 25, we see that Amaziah entered into battle without the blessing of the Lord. With every vision, there is something that God wants us to establish in a territory that is occupied by the enemy, and we need the Lord to cover us and be with us every step of the way. Mercifully, God provided Amaziah with a man of God to warn him of his misstep before it was too late. It is a blessing to know that God will place people in our lives that love and care about us and care about what we are trying to accomplish. There has been a time when I have been weary and wanted to give up on the vision, and someone either confirms the vision or encourages me just at that time.

> But there came a man of God to him, saying, O king, let not the army of Israel go with thee; for the Lord is not with Israel, to wit, with all the children of Ephraim. But if thou wilt go, do it; be strong for the battle: God shall make thee fall before the enemy: for God hath power to help, and to cast down. And Amaziah said to the man of God, But what shall we do for the hundred talents which I have given to the army of Israel? And the man of God answered, The Lord is able to give thee much more than this. (2 Chronicles 25:7–9)

Fortunately, King Amaziah obeyed the man of God even though the people were upset that he did not go to battle when they thought that he should. When Amaziah later moved into strategic warfare with the blessing of the Lord, the battle was won. However, King Amaziah failed to deal with his tendency toward apostasy, and he set up an altar to other gods, even though the Lord had shown Himself strong in the battle against the Edomites. He began to worship the gods of the children of Seir, meaning a he-goat, the god of flesh and rebellion.

After the death of his father Amaziah, King Uzziah began to reign. The Scriptures state the following:

> And he sought God in the days of Zechariah, who had understanding in the visions of God: and as long as he sought the LORD, God made him to prosper. (2 Chronicles 26:5)

In spite of the ambivalent legacy of his forefathers, Uzziah remembered that the Lord God was the God of Judah, and he sought counsel from the prophet of God. Uzziah was strong, and the Scriptures indicate that he won many battles and that his name was great in the land because he strengthened himself exceedingly. He was encouraged in the plan and will of God concerning him.

> And Uzziah prepared for them throughout all the host shields, and spears, and helmets, and habergeons, and bows, and slings to cast stones. And he made in Jerusalem engines, invented by cunning men, to be on the towers and upon the bulwarks, to shoot arrows and great stones withal. And his name spread far abroad; for he was marvelously helped, till he was strong. (2 Chronicles 26:14–15)

There was an individual plan, and each person in the battle had to know his or her position and be properly equipped. Then there was a corporate plan that protected the city and the overall vision: engines or warlike machines that shot arrows and great stones.

There are some positive lessons to be learned from Uzziah; he had an insightful (and bafflingly simple) battle strategy: he equipped his soldiers. They had to engage their faith, believe the word of God concerning the vision, and be fully assured of their relationship with the Lord. That assurance will certainly be tested while waiting for the vision. His corporate team was innovative and creative; the plan was to address any opposition at the root. An opposition may be set up in the camp or outside the camp. The enemy is not going to just let us implement the plan of God in the earth realm without a fight; we must prepare for war, through prayer and intercession. The vision requires the visionary to be surrounded by wise individuals; one person cannot do it by himself or herself.

However, when God calls you into leadership and He gives you a vision concerning His heart for the region, nation, or global community, you need to ensure that you maintain correct alignment in your worship and relationship with Him. Uzziah thought that he could bypass the proper protocol of true worship of the Lord. He allowed his popularity to become his ultimate calamity. It is easy to believe that you are special because God is speaking to you, but the Lord is no respecter of persons: He seeks the true worshipers.

> But when he was strong, his heart was lifted up to his destruction: for he transgressed against the Lord his God, and went into the temple of the Lord to burn incense upon the altar of incense. And Azariah the priest went in after him, and with him fourscore priests of the LORD, that were valiant men: And they withstood Uzziah the king, and said unto him, It appertaineth not unto thee, Uzziah, to burn incense unto the LORD, but to the priests the sons of Aaron, that are consecrated to burn incense: go out of the sanctuary; for thou hast trespassed; neither shall it be for thine honour from the LORD God. Then Uzziah was wroth, and had a censer in his hand to burn incense: and while he was wroth with the priests, the leprosy even rose up in his forehead before the priests in the house of the LORD, from beside the incense altar. And Azariah the chief priest, and all the priests, looked upon him, and, behold, he was leprous in his forehead, and they thrust him out from thence; yea, himself hasted also to go out, because the LORD had smitten him. And Uzziah the king was a leper unto the day of his death, and dwelt in a several house, being a leper; for he was cut off from the house of the LORD: and Jotham his son was over the king's house, judging the people of the land. Now the rest of the acts of Uzziah, first and last, did Isaiah the prophet, the son of Amoz, write. (2 Chronicles 26:16–22)

Uzziah dishonored the temple of the Lord, and we will likely come across individuals who will dishonor the vision that God has given us. Bishop Tudor Bismark, in his book entitled *The Spirit of Honor*, states that anyone sowing a seed of dishonor will inhibit a spiritual breakthrough; this spirit of dishonor must be dealt with immediately, no matter how long that individual has been a part of the ministry (Bismark, 2008).

The Lord essentially spat in Uzziah's face, and Uzziah lived his later years shut up as a leper. Bishop Tudor Bismark argues the following:

- When God spits in the face of a ministry, it will suffer spiritual leprosy or isolation.

- Leprosy is a disease that attacks the nervous system and causes both deformity and the loss of limbs (such that you cannot feel anymore).

- When this spiritual leprosy occurs, you lose sensitivity to the Spirit of God, the times, the seasons, your gifts, and the people in your life.

There is so much at stake when we dishonor the Lord, the vision, and the visionary. We cannot come into our place of destiny until this "dis-ease" is dealt with. I strongly recommend that you read Bishop Bismark's book *The Spirit of Honor* to further understand these concepts.

During the year in which Uzziah died, the prophet Isaiah had a vision. (Isaiah exercised his prophetic calling during Uzziah's reign and continued through the next three reigns of kings.)

> In the year that king Uzziah died I saw also the Lord sitting upon a throne, high and lifted up, and his train filled the temple. (Isaiah 6:1)

The season changed after Uzziah's death. His son Jotham reigned as king. Jotham's name means "Jehovah is perfect." He did what was right in the sight of the Lord, and there was a season of open vision again. Isaiah was able to see the glory of the Lord. The atmosphere must be set in terms of recognizing and submitting to the perfection and sufficiency of the Lord in all that He requires us to do.

The Jezebel Spirit

A vision will lead to the manifestation of the divine will of God in the earth, and it starts with a prophetic utterance. Wherever the prophetic anointing resides, the spirit of Jezebel can also be found lurking, waiting for an occasion to manifest. Jezebel was a Phoenician princess who married Ahab king of Israel. Jezebel was an idolatrous woman who opposed God's ways. Jezebel's primary focus was to slay the true prophets of the Lord God of Israel by castrating them, rendering them ineffective in the kingdom of God (1 Kings 18:4 and 19 and 1 Kings 19:1–2). Elijah was a major prophet during that time that opposed Jezebel; she desired to kill him also, and because of the sins of the nation, Elijah declared to King Ahab that there would be no rain for a significant period. Elijah challenged the false prophets of Jezebel on Mount Carmel in 1 Kings 18,

> And Ahab told Jezebel all that Elijah had done, and withal how he had slain all the prophets with the sword. Then Jezebel sent a messenger unto Elijah, saying, So let the gods do to me, and more also, if I make not thy life as the life of one of them by to morrow about this time. (1 King 19:1–2)

As I have walked through vision development, I have had to deal with this spirit periodically. In the Bible, Ahab and Jezebel lived in a place called Jezreel, which was in the land of Samaria. That land was given to one of the twelve tribes of Israel known as Issachar. In 1 Chronicles 12:32, we see that Issachar was the tribe known for flowing in revelation. They were the ones who understood the "times and seasons of God" and what Israel, the promised people of God, should do. The Jezebel spirit set up her throne in the "Land of Revelation." Jezebel's assignment is to hinder the voice of the prophets through occupying that territory. It is imperative that we are clearly aware of the following:

1. Jezebel is a demonic influence.

2. The "spirit of Jezebel" existed before Jezebel the queen, but she was so influenced by it that she became its namesake (see 1 Kings 16 and Revelation 2:20).

3. The spirit seeks control through manipulation.

4. It has a deep hatred for spiritual authority that walks in the true love of God; it is her greatest enemy.

5. The spirit pursues power through manipulation.

6. The spirit uses emotional pressure, witchcraft, and obsessive sensuality in the pursuit of power.

7. She will look for an inroad and attempt to use subtle persuasion to be influential in the leadership team, getting close to those in control. She will then use this position to dominate the headship and the direction of the ministry.

8. The spirit refuses to *cohabitate* with someone whom it cannot dominate or control.

9. The spirit plants seeds of doubt in others and attempts to use its power of influence over others to accomplish its goals and control its environment. "So she wrote letters in Ahab's name, and sealed them with his seal, and sent the letters unto the elders and to the nobles that were in his city, dwelling with Naboth" (1 Kings 21:8).

10. The spirit is often associated with pleasure, especially sexual pleasure.

11. It is the leading power behind the birth of witchcraft in Britain and the United States among our young people—certain kinds of music or movies that contain subliminal messages that may lead to immoral behavior, Internet pornography, and psychic hotlines.

12. She leads the Church into spiritual adultery.

13. She often manifests in the most spiritual people. Revelations 2:20 talks about the residency of the Jezebel spirit in the church of Thyatira. The scriptures says that she called herself a prophetess, which taught and seduced Christ's servants to commit fornication as well as eat things sacrificed unto idols. Her demonic deception usually result in the condemnation and burdening of those in her care.

14. This spirit causes demonic depression and loss of vision. When she threatened Elijah, he became a coward and fled to the desert, anxious, depressed, and miserable (self-pity). He even begged God to kill him. Prior to that threat, Elijah enjoyed supernatural protection from God for seven years. Why would she have so much influence? She appeared to have influence over the King Ahab, the ruling authority over the region; Elijah did not feel that he would be safe or protected in that region. Jezebel had a history of getting what she wanted and instilled fear and intimidation in others.

15. She attacks key leaders. Sometimes it takes effort just to breathe because joy departs, spiritual life seems irrelevant, and demonic voices will echo that something is wrong with you. Under the influence of Jezebel, one may even experience unreasonable anxiety, fear, tragedy, or death.

16. The spirit wants to paralyze you until you withdraw.

Her Goal

Every visionary walks in a prophetic anointing. Jezebel is constantly working to slay the true prophets of the Lord Jesus by castrating them, cutting off their ability to produce seed or vision, and rendering them ineffective in the kingdom of God (1 Kings 18 and 19).

In Revelation 2:20, we see the Jezebel spirit residing in the church of Thyatira. The church of Thyatira was a church that had some excellent qualities: love, faith, service, patient endurance, and greater works. This church also had the following:

1. Power over the nations – The church was in a set place at a set time with legal authority from heaven.

2. Victory over the enemy – The church was the ranking authority in the region, speaking, decreeing, declaring, and legislating the will of God in the region.

3. The morning star – More importantly, the church had the power of Jesus Christ as its covering and backing.

Fear that Paralyzes

Jezebel operates in the realm of insecurities. She will continually challenge God's Word in your life in an effort to dislodge you from your faith. Jezebel flows well in four main atmospheres:

1. fear – panic, alarm, apprehension
2. insecurity – lack of self-confidence
3. frustration – aggravation, irritation, disappointment, dissatisfaction
4. confusion – misunderstanding, uncertainty

Fear emerges out of intimidation, which emerges out of her mother, Jezebel. Fear is a demonic interference that hinders your destiny or assignment. In such cases, the spiritual law or principle of "the three threaded cord" must be applied to your life: power, love, and a sound mind. You must understand that deliverance from fear is an investment in your future; you will gain more than what you give up, and you will not be easily broken. Elijah not only knew what God could do, but he saw the manifestation of the Almighty God on Mount Carmel when He consumed a watered sacrifice with fire. Elijah then killed the false prophets of Baal and revealed those who were walking in truth, but he still ran and became suicidal when Jezebel threatened him. Fear will pursue you in an attempt to kill you or take you out before your time. Elijah had not yet mentored a successor. He had to face Jezebel before he could move on to the next assignment.

Fear may also cause you to operate alone. Fear is the difference between you functioning as a worthless commodity or a priceless commodity in the body of Christ. When you are alone, you begin to hear voices. The Lord will often call us into places alone with Him for a season, but we must recognize when the season is over and then realign or connect with like-minded believers. We also have to be careful of the spirit of hurt or offense. Jezebel will cause deep emotional hurts and wounds in order to gain an inroad and strategically set you up for the kill. We must become aware of our weaknesses and hurts, get healing or counseling if necessary, or even withdraw from the frontline for a season. Most individuals who operate in the spirit of Jezebel have been wounded.

We must be focused and aware of God's will when developing a vision. The moment we begin to doubt the Word of God, that doubt produces an open door for the enemy to further compound our fears. Jezebel uses the seduction of flattering words, words that confirm our negative thinking, and smooth sayings to gain entrance into our emotions. Compliments for the purpose of manipulation are from the wrong spirit, and such compliments indicate a release of witchcraft or control. The door of your spirit can be opened by first seducing you through your soul: your mind, will, emotions, conscience, and imagination. You will know when this spirit is at work because you will feel uneasy. We must walk in a spirit of discernment so that we do not operate solely in our emotions or make decisions from the soulish realm.

Qualifications and Principles for Dealing with Jezebel

To gain an understanding and to effectively deal with the spirit of Jezebel, it is imperative to examine Elijah's qualifications and why he was successful in dealing with this spirit. I identify a nine-fold anointing that Elijah walked in; we can cultivate this anointing to effectively tear down this spirit. They are as follows:

- Prophetic Office – The primary role of prophets is to receive new divine revelation from God and to speak it into the atmosphere.

- Every great prophet is an intercessor, and every great intercessor should have the spirit of a prophet.

- Cannot pray the problem, but instead, speak the solution and judgment.

- Declared no rain or dew – No blessings in a place where the will of God is being violated

- Turned eastward – Stay in a place of revelation, ears always in tune with that of God.

○ He hid in the brook Cherith – This signified a place of covenant or alliance with God.

○ Elijah drank from the brook – He ultimately relied on his covenant relationship for safety and security and guidance

○ Ravens fed him bread and flesh in the morning and evening – Raven can mean be darkened and grow dusky at sundown. Even in a dark place, of doubt and fear, the Lord will cover us, protect us, and feed us spiritually so that we do not get weak in our faith, that may be done through the love and guidance of other, through praying, reading the word of God, revelation, etc.

○ He went to Zaraphath of Zidon, a place of protection and peace, where he was sustained. Sometimes, the thing that is sustaining you will dry up or even die, but God will revive it again (the widow's son died and came back to life). New life is coming!

Definition of "Sustain"

To keep in, to maintain, to measure, to make provision

After killing the false prophets, Elijah ran to Jezreel (meaning "God will sow").

1. Be recognized by the spirit of Jezebel as one who has come to trouble the sins or distractions that will hinder the people's relationship with the Lord. We must walk with spiritual authority.

2. Call the people to correct worship. Aligned adoration of God will release the blessing.

3. Pray with the correct motive (1 Kings 18:37). Call down fire from heaven, the promises of God for the region.

4. Do not compromise – Elijah slew all the false prophets (in other words, do not listen to any voices contrary to the will and vision of the Lord).

5. Call rain – Change the atmosphere so all can eat or benefit from the promises of God.

6. Stay on course to the correct destination. Elijah ran to Jezreel, which means "God will sow" and represents a place of promise and prosperity.

Jehu the conqueror, whose name means "Jehovah is He," is our example of what it takes to defeat the spirit of Jezebel (1 Kings 21:23, 2 Kings 9:5–7, and 2 Kings 9:37). Jehu was referred to as a commander.

- ○ He had a commanding anointing on his life.
- ○ He was not a passive believer of Jehovah.
- ○ He was a man of spiritual rank, strength, and fortitude.

God sent his prophet to anoint Jehu with a powerful warring anointing. We must work collaboratively to slay Jezebel:

> And it shall come to pass, that him that escapeth the sword of Hazael shall Jehu_slay: and him that escapeth from the sword of Jehu shall Elisha slay. (1 Kings 19:17)

We must operate in a threefold process:

1. Hazael ("God has seen") – Discernment.
2. Jehu ("Jehovah is He") – Authority; Jehu confronted the ruling authority which was a corrupt religious and political system.
3. Elisha ("God of supplication or of riches") – Power, provision, and inheritance.

We cannot fear Jezebel. She can be killed, she has been killed, and she will be killed. We set the spiritual atmosphere so God can do the killing.

> And he that overcometh, and keepeth my works unto the end, to him will I give power over the nations: And he shall rule them with a rod of iron; as the vessels of a potter shall they be broken to shivers: even as I received of my Father. And I will give him the morning star. (Revelation 2:26–28)

I believe that the Church has experienced many encounters with Jezebel so that we can recognize her and conquer her. Training was done in our own camps so that we can apply the skills outside of the camp. You will have no ministry to the nations until you learn how to conquer Jezebel, her prophets, and her spiritual children who attack your vision and ministry. Many territorial spirits will try to attack the vision, but we must learn to dominate them using the strategy of wisdom and worship. Know your enemy, and continue to worship the Almighty God. The purpose of kingdom visions must be twofold: meeting a need and bringing people back to the Lord. On Mount Carmel, Elijah prayed, "Hear me, O LORD, hear me, that this people may know that thou art the LORD God, and that thou hast turned their heart back again" (1 Kings 18:37).

Much has been written on the spirits of Ahab, Jezebel, and their daughter Athaliah. However, I would caution you to also look out for the spirit of Ahab and Athaliah, as they can greatly hinder vision. Once you identify them, you need to be aware of their characteristics and be skilled in dealing with them. The spirit of Jezebel comes to hinder that vision, and Athaliah is a seed killer or a dream killer. I prepared a chart for you to identify these spirits at a quick glance. I pray it is as useful to you as it is to me:

Hindering Spirit	Characteristics	Tools for Dismantling Them
Ahab – brother/kindred, chief, father, principal	1. Weak character 2. Covetous 3. Overly merciful or overly legalistic 4. Fear of rejection 5. Low self-esteem	1. Move in spiritual rank, strength, and fortitude
Jezebel – island, dwelling, residence, habitation	1. Promotes perverse worship 2. Manipulation 3. Control 4. Intimidation 5. Stagnation	1. Repent 2. Offer God true worship 3. Stand upon the promises of God 4. Be courageous and strong

	5. Character, spiritual, or literal assassination 6. Operates in false prophecy 7. Promotes fear and discouragement 8. Promotes rebellion against the will and Word of Almighty God	
Athaliah – Jah has seized	1. Seed and dream killer—destroys the generations and generational blessings and inheritance 2. Negativity 3. "Take over" spirit 4. Causes doubt regarding the Word and covenantal promises of God	1. Protect the seed and dream—be wise about when and to whom you reveal sensitive information (see 2 Chronicles 22:10–12) 2. Take out this spirit with the sword and Word—then revival will begin (see 2 Chronicles 23:12–15) 3. Implement legitimate church government and authority structures

We cannot allow any negative spirits to influence us. Sometimes, it can be so easy for spirits to attach themselves to us, and we have to be very careful that the doors to our wounds and insecurities are closed, that we are healed and walking in confidence in the will of God. "Cast not away therefore your confidence, which hath great recompence of reward" (Hebrews 10:35). I have learned that a lack of confidence is a sign of unrepentance and unforgiveness. Confidence comes with deliverance, conquests, and spiritual exploits. It is imperative during this season that we have a strong belief system and full assurance in our assignments.

Part Two

A Guided Tour through Vision Development

And the LORD answered me, and said, Write the vision, and make it plain upon tables, that he may run that readeth it.

—Habakkuk 2:2

Chapter 5

Purpose of Heart

The prophet Daniel was a young man who was in captivity in Jerusalem during the reign of King Jehoiakim. King Nebuchadnezzar of Babylon besieged the city of Jerusalem and instructed one of his chief servants to bring some young men to his palace: "Children in whom was no blemish, but well-favored, and skillful in all wisdom, and cunning in knowledge, and understanding science, and such as had ability in them to stand in the king's palace, and whom they might teach the learning and the tongue of the Chaldeans" (Daniel 1:4). Daniel was one of these young men. When we talk about Daniel, we often see his prophetic anointing and neglect to discuss his gifts of vision, wisdom, and insight. Daniel was able to understand the purpose, meaning, and intent of the times.

Purpose

The first time that the word "purpose" is mentioned in the Bible is in Ruth 2:16: "And let fall also some of the handfuls of *purpose* for her, and leave them, that she may glean them, and rebuke her not." The Hebrew definition of the word "purpose" in this particular passage is to drop or strip; to plunder, let fall, make self a prey; or to make or take as a spoil.

The purpose of your heart will often be the determining factor of whether or not the Lord releases a vision. To become a visionary, you need to correctly position your heart. We need the anointing of the Lord to do any given task well; the anointing helps us to understand and walk in our purpose and operate in our rank of authority. The anointing gives you the authority to drop something, strip something, plunder something, make something fall or come to an end, causing the kingdom of darkness to be dethroned in a particular place or region or take the spoils of something. When developing a vision, you have to know the intended assignment or desired results and the level of anointing required for that hour or that season.

The first time that the word *purpose* is mentioned in the Bible is in Ruth 2:16 "And let fall also some of the handfuls of *purpose* for her, and leave them, that she may glean them, and rebuke her not." When looking at purpose, it is imperative to also understand the Greek definition of the word. In ancient Greek, the word translated into English as "purpose" means a setting forth or proposal (intention), especially the *shewbread* (in the Temple) as exposed before God. When understanding purpose, we especially need to understand the significance of the showbread in the Old Testament Temple as that which is exposed before God. When God develops a vision, the visionary becomes the sacrifice; they will often be a blessing to others. Their dreams will be exchanged for the dreams of heaven. A God-given vision is always bigger than the visionary, and it can sometimes be a heavy burden that keeps that individual in a constant place of prayer and supplication.

Secondly, the visionary, like the showbread, will often be broken and served to the priest. However, when King David and his men were hungry, they ate the showbread, "How he entered into the house of God, and did eat the shewbread, which was not lawful for him to eat, neither for them which were with him, but only for the priests?" (Matthew 12:4). Showbread was known as the "bread of the presence of God." It stayed in God's presence, continually showing the Lord's desire to fellowship with humankind. We see in the New Testament that the Lord still desires to fellowship with us, "Behold, I stand at the door, and knock: if any man hear my voice, and open the door, I will come in to him, and will sup with him, and he with me" (Revelations 3:20). When we fulfill our purpose, we aim to draw others closer to the Lord; we are served to the people, servant-leaders, even though the people will not always see or agree with you. The

Greek meaning for "purpose" is in the "middle voice" and means to place before oneself or to exhibit (demonstrative). The visionary is the intermediate between the Lord and the people, the community, or the nation. The "showbread" is known as *lechem ha'panim*, which means "bread of the face" or "bread of the presence (of God)." It is also called the "continual bread" (Numbers 4:7), "continual shew-bread" (1 Chronicles 2:4), or "bread of the row" (or "arrangement," 1 Chronicles 9:32). The loaves were mixed and kneaded outside of the courtyard. God will not trust His heart and mind to just anyone. A visionary has to be processed.

The anointing for purpose comes from the following:

○ When God wants to step into a place, it comes to heal, restore, and promote.

○ To discover the hidden things.

○ To work with the angels of the church for the edification and purification of the body and rebuilding of the nation. It will move towards redemption, restoration, and reconciliation.

It was imperative that we have a clear understanding of our purpose to receive the vision of God. What we have purposed in your heart will lead to vision, which in turn will lead to the fulfillment of purpose.

The Seer

> And of the children of Issachar, which were men that had understanding of the times, to know what Israel ought to do; the heads of them were two hundred; and all their brethren were at their commandment. (1 Chronicles 12:32)

We are in a season in which the Lord is speaking clearly to leaders who dare to implement His vision in the earth. The word of God is living and when it is spoken it sets things into motion to accomplish what it was sent to do. As we begin to read the book of Daniel, we see that Daniel was one of the "children in whom was no blemish, but well favored, and skillful in all wisdom, and cunning in knowledge, and understanding science, and such as had ability in them to stand in the king's palace, and whom they might teach the learning and the tongue of the Chaldeans" (Daniel 1:4). We see in this one scripture that Daniel had a nine-fold gifting that qualified him to be a visionary:

1. *No blemish* – This meaning could be twofold, without spots or stains physically or morally. Daniel operated from a place of purity.

2. *Well Favored – a view (the act of seeing); also an appearance (the thing seen) or (mental) a vision.* It was evident to the people around Daniel by the way he carried himself that he was in his set place at the set time. His appearance commanded respect.

3. *Skillful – circumspect and hence, intelligent; to teach, instruct, and prosper.* He had acquired the ability to teach others.

4. *Wise – having the power of discerning and judging properly as to what is true or right; possessing discernment, judgment, or discretion.* Daniel knew that God was eternal and that what came out of *kairos* time needed to be manifested in *chronos* time. He understood that knowledge had to be placed in the correct chronological timeframe. He was articulate and could relate to those around him, regardless of whether they were superiors or subordinates

5. *Cunning in knowledge – to observe, recognize, see, advise, answer, and comprehend. Knowledge related to light.* Daniel was able to bring illumination to social and political concerns in the kingdom.

6. *Understanding – diligent, discern, or perceive.* With understanding comes the release of the prophetic anointing.

7. *Science – intelligence, consciousness, knowledge, or thought.* Daniel was able to relate to a multidimensional world: the

visible and the invisible. It is impossible to make a decision about one dimension without affecting other dimensions, which we will discuss further in this chapter.

8. *The ability to stand before kings and those in authority* – Daniel knew his time and his season, and he did not allow himself to be intimidated by the status of the king. By the time God sets you before kings, you need to recognize that you are the right person for the assignment; it is not the time for false humility. Be confident, open your mouth, and speak; they are waiting for you.

9. *A teachable spirit* – We need to be open to grow and learn in knowledge and wisdom daily.

The book of Daniel is loaded with so many strategies and requirements for a visionary. Daniel was careful about what he ate. As a result, the Scriptures say that Daniel was ten times better than all the magicians and astrologers that were in the palace of the king. The sons of Issachar were astrologers. In the New Testament era, astrology is seen as a negative concept associated with horoscopes. However, during the Old Testament era, there was a distinction between God-commissioned astrologers and those who were workers of magic or witchcraft. In the Scriptures, the number 10 represents judgment. The vision that the Lord gives you is the final authority on a particular matter. A vision brings judgment on *what is* and legislates *what will be*. Like Daniel, we have to be careful what we allow into our spirits and what we consume or dwell upon. We have to surround ourselves with people that will speak life into the vision that we are carrying.

Vision is also dependent on unlocking the Word of God prophetically, discover what God is saying to us now; correct interpretation is vital. Daniel 1:17 identifies four qualifications of a visionary: "As for these four children, God gave them knowledge and skill in all learning and wisdom: and Daniel had understanding in all visions and dreams." It is imperative as visionaries that we have a clear understanding of the meaning of these key concepts. As I began to study the giftings that Daniel operated in, it was interesting to see that sometimes we lose the depth of the meaning of these words in the translation from Hebrew to English. I thought that I would share the Hebrew meaning with you as it opened my eyes to the level of gifting we carry when we walk in these gifts; they are as follows:

1. Knowledge (*madda*) – The biblical meaning is intelligence, consciousness, or thought. This word is also translated as science.

2. Skill in all learning (*skal cepher*) – This phrase speaks of an expert, instructor, or teacher in writing or recording a book.

3. Wisdom (*chokmah*) – To be wise in mind, word, or act; it also means to operate with skill and wit.

4. Understanding (*biyn*) – The ability to separate thoughts mentally, attend, consider, be cunning, be diligent, direct, discern, or be eloquent. In the process of developing an understanding on a particular issue, inform, or instruct in the subject area.

As we read through this verse and gain the Hebrew understanding of each concept, it becomes very apparent that it is dangerous to have visions and dreams with no understanding. As I explore the book of Daniel further, I find additional qualifications of a visionary, which are as follows:

o   *Heart condition* – Must have a heart for the things of God.

o   *Diet* – Correct interpretations come when we feed our spirits with the Word of God, and correct alignment in our relationship with the Lord is essential.

o   *Might* – In Isaiah 11:2, we see that the spirit of might is a God quality, which is a spirit of force, strength, power, and victory. "Might" also means mastery, or having dominion over some things.

o   *Obedience* – We may not understand everything that we see, but the Apostle Paul declared in Acts 26:19, "Whereupon, O king Agrippa, I was not disobedient unto the heavenly vision."

Interpretation of Visions and Dreams

It is imperative to determine what kingdom someone is representing when a vision is being interpreted or implemented. The book of Daniel identifies four other sources of dream interpretation, which are as follows:

1. magicians

2. astrologers

3. sorcerers

4. Chaldeans

Incorrect interpretation or a lack of remembrance of the word of the Lord has serious consequences, and there will be certain destruction and a foul odor coming from what we attempt to offer the Lord.

We must also remember that dreams and visions are important and can be stolen in the night season, during the challenges or the death of the vision. In Daniel 2:5, "The king answered and said to the Chaldeans, The thing is gone from me: if ye will not make known unto me the dream, with the interpretation thereof, ye shall be cut in pieces, and your houses shall be made a dunghill." Night visions, which can occur when we are half awake or half asleep, are powerful, and we must understand that it is the assignment of the underworld to destroy visions and dreams (Daniel 2:19–24). A night vision includes that which God reveals to you in a dark season of your life, your community, or the church. It is vital that we grab it and hold on to it; we must write them down as soon as we come to a place of consciousness. There have been times when I think I will remember them in the morning, and I forget them when I go back to sleep. They will bring light or illumination to a dark season; it can and will change the course of history.

When unfolding a dream or vision, we have to be careful about lying and corrupt words. We need the office of wisdom to be reinstated in the body of Christ. The king had wise men around him in Daniel 2:12; wisdom is a gift and an office. Sometimes you may not know what is deep in your spirit until you communicate with someone who is connected with the Lord, someone who can pull that spiritual reality into your soulish realm (mind, will, emotions, conscience, and imagination). It is heaven that reveals secrets (Daniel 2:28).

We must start with the premise that a vision is certainly going to come to pass; it is not a hope or a pipe dream (Daniel 2:29). The implementation of a vision is about strategy and timelines, as well as hindrances and opposition. This is known in the business world as a SWOT analysis. It is imperative for any organization to be able to conduct an analysis of its overall situation and stated initiatives. The SWOT (strengths, weaknesses, opportunities, threats) analysis identifies the internal strengths and weaknesses of an organization in relation to a specific focus of study, as well as the external opportunities and threats that the organization may face. The analysis has proven to be beneficial in assisting organizations with addressing any areas of concern in terms of pursuing and achieving their visions and goals. This a useful tool that churches and individuals can use in the development of their vision.

The vision will bring God glory and will cause the believer and unbeliever alike to bow. It is important to remember that we are often going to be dealing with people who do not know God or people who have forgotten who He is and what He can do. When God calls you, the opposition has no power over you!

The Lord is no respecter of persons when it comes to the impartation of a vision. In fact, God will often use the least likely. We must remember the following:

1. The Most High rules in the kingdom of man.

2. He gives it to whomsoever He wills.

3. The Lord will often set the basest and humblest individuals over the kingdom.

4. The Spirit of the Lord gives us the interpretation of visions and dreams. We must be careful not to be boastful about what the Lord accomplishes through us.

5. The interpretation is the Word of the Lord; it is therefore settled and established.

Correct interpretation leads to blessings, as we see in Daniel 2:6: "But if ye shew the dream, and the interpretation thereof, ye shall receive of me gifts and rewards and great honour: therefore shew me the dream, and the interpretation thereof." Similarly, Daniel 5:7 says, "Whosoever shall read this writing, and shew me the interpretation thereof, shall be clothed with scarlet, and have a chain of gold about his neck, and shall be the third ruler in the kingdom." As we can see from the above passages, the blessings of correct interpretation can include the following:

- gifts
- rewards
- great honor
- covering
- wealth
- governance

Once we receive an interpretation from the Lord, we must make declarations over the vision. Knowledge of what God is saying brings illumination, and correct interpretation dissolves doubts. Like Daniel, we must have understanding, wisdom, and an excellent spirit. He was also a faithful, steadfast intercessor. Prayer is required during this season; we must be diligent enough to locate the vision in chronological time and identify the specific mandates of the vision. Sometimes the vision of God will take your breath and your strength away. We cannot fear, but rather, we must be strong and walk in peace as we move with clear direction.

In Hosea 12:10, we see that God uses similitude and speaks in visions through the prophets. As visionaries, we have now stepped into another realm. The Lord will bring us out by a prophet (Hosea 12:13), so let the prophetic leaders arise. The season in which God's people are destroyed for the lack of knowledge and light (Hosea 4:6) is over.

Dimensions

What is string theory and why are we addressing this concept in the book? I will provide a brief synopsis of the theory; it is necessary for us to understand string theory. String theory attempt to answer the question, "What is the world made from?" Physicists who study energy and matter define string as an anything longer in length than its width (Bernatowicz, 2011). Our clothing is made up of strings; cable wires are considered string, DNA is called strings, as well as matters that we cannot see. Some scientists believe that everything is made up of string. The theory was originally developed in the 1970s, which was focused on one-dimension objects and has evolved over the years as a multidimensional theory (Zimmerman Jones and Robbins, 2016). String theory can be complex as it involves higher dimensions and other universes. This theory is distinct from classical physics, the theories of relativity, and quantum gravity (the study of the smallest objects in nature).

Some physicist holds the view that there are ten dimensions or even up to twenty-six dimensions. All physicists have long established that we live in a world defined by three spatial dimensions (perceived as physical and tangible) and a fourth dimension of duration or time. This information suggests that it only takes three numbers to pin-point a specific physical location at any given moment in the earth realm; these coordinates are described as longitude, latitude, and altitude. The coordinates represent the dimensions of length, width, and height (or depth). When a time stamp is placed on those coordinates; objects can be pinpointed in time also. As previously stated, in our three-dimensional physical world, we also have an additional fourth dimension rolled into it called time:

1. length
2. width
3. depth
4. time

I first learned about string theory through the series of messages on "Dimensions" ministered by Bishop Tudor Bismark. This concept is critical to understanding the visionary's readiness to walk out a vision, as well as the vision's location in time. As we continue to develop this concept, it is essential to understand the possibilities that open up in terms of the development and analysis of a vision. We need to be able to travel back and forth in time in the realm of the spirit through intercessory prayer and faith. There are many people that are physicists, researchers, mystics, philosophers, astrophysicists, astronomers, astrologers, spiritual leaders, astronauts, engineers, psychics, etc. argue that we need to understand how the universe functions. Some even believe that there are in fact several universes, each with its own progressions of dimensional reality and possible outcomes. Some scientists expand upon the traditional four-dimensional reality to encapsulate ten dimensions (and others suggest even more). These ten dimensions, in theory, are actually the sum of all universes and all of their possible outcomes (Moskowitz, 2012). Understanding these ten dimensions may help scientists begin to develop a unified theory that can thoroughly explain all physical phenomena (Bismark, 2012).

When dealing with spiritual dimensions, Bishop Tudor Bismark advocates that the following ten components are necessary. The Lord began to speak to me about these ten components in the framework of vision implementation; I have examined these components from this perspective.

Ten Dimensions

1. *Faith*

    The biblical meaning of the word "faith" is associated with trustworthiness and truth. The Scriptures declare, "Behold, his soul which is lifted up is not upright in him: but the just shall live by his faith" (Habakkuk 2:4). In the season of vision development, great faith is needed. We are required to stand on the Word of God, whether it is the written Word or a "right now" Word from the Lord; we must live by that Word. What the Lord has spoken can be trusted; it is truth, and we can legislate it to be so. We cannot veer left or right from the Word of God, but we must wait for it to come to pass.

2. *Light*

The Hebrew definition of "light" is illumination, happiness, bright, clear, morning, sun, the break of day, glorious, or set on fire. I love the Scriptures that declare the authority in the creative voice of God: "And God said, Let there be light: and there was light. And God saw the light, that it was good: and God divided the light from the darkness" (Genesis 1:3–4). In this season, God is bringing illumination to His word or directives concerning the visions that He has given us. We must wait on the light and not try to grope in the darkness. This may take much time in prayer and waiting on the Lord. During the waiting period, the Lord is preparing things behind the scenes, including processing us for the promise. The light will bring joy as the new day begins to dawn.

3. *Wisdom and Knowledge*

Wisdom is simply being skillful. Exodus 28:3 states, "And thou shalt speak unto all that are wise hearted, whom I have filled with the spirit of wisdom, that they may make Aaron's garments to consecrate him, that he may minister unto me in the priest's office." As we begin to move with wisdom, we will move with the creative and innovative anointing of God. The anointing that brings clarity to direction and priorities will be imparted to the visionary.

4. *Revelation and Truth*

Revelation means the disclosure, appearing, or manifestation. It is awesome that revelation and truth are together. When we receive revelation, we are able to move in confidence that we are operating in the truth of the word or the directive of God; God covers His truth. It is sure and unchangeable. Because we are visionaries, the Lord is revealing His secrets to us. Revelation is simply a manifestation of what is already established in the heavens—the intended will of the Lord for the earth realm. Romans 16:25 states, "Now to him that is of power to establish you according to my gospel, and the preaching of Jesus Christ, according to the revelation of the mystery, which was kept secret since the world began."

5. *Power*

   Power indicates firmness, force, might, strength, or wealth. We have an assurance that no matter how dark the night may be or how deep the roots of the vision have to go, the vision will be birthed and it will produce; we will push forward in power no matter the obstacles we may face.

6. *Life*

   The Hebrew definition for "life" means to be fresh, strong, congregation, running, springing, or truth. Life is a distinction of organic, living organisms, or inorganic dead objects. Life is manifested through reproduction and growth. When I looked up the Hebrew definition of "life," it was interesting to discover that the vision will bring freshness to the church, the community, and the region. Vision is needed in order to bring life or enhance life; it will eliminate the old (or rebuild the old) and develop the new.

7. *King*

   The definition of "king" is royal, reign, ascend to the throne, take counsel, consult, or rule. As visionaries, we govern, legislate, and judge on behalf of heaven; we also move in the judicial authority, power, and anointing of the Lord Jesus Christ. The Scriptures declare that God "hast made us unto our God kings and priests: and we shall reign on the earth" (Revelation 5:10).

8. *Prosperity*

The Hebrew definition of "prosperity" is beautiful, best, better, bountiful, cheerful, at ease, favor, wealth, or welfare. What is birthed in the divine plan of God will be prosperous in its time or season. What an awesome promise and legacy! We live in a world devoid of spiritual wealth, living in spiritual bankruptcy. The vision will bring balance back to our society.

9. *Healing and Miracles*

Every vision from heaven is designed to make room for the greater works, to show the world the power of the true and living God, Jesus Christ the Lord of heaven; there is none before Him and none coming after Him. The implementation of the vision will bring healing to a people, a community, and a nation.

10. *Worship and Prophecy*

I believe that in this season, worship is a critical component to engaging heaven. While the church may understand it, it has not always been practiced. Worship invokes the presence of God and creates an atmosphere where the Lord is welcome and His spirit can rest and minister. Worship ministers to the Lord who in turn ministers to the worshiper. It is imperative to attract the Lord and not just the blessing; we beckon the Reviver, not just a revival. The fragrance of worship begins to eradicate the ways of the old nature, as we pursue becoming more like Christ. Worship has a multifold purpose—it also shakes the enemy off his throne in the region and causes turmoil in the underworld. The enemy hates the worship of Almighty God, and he tries to steal our worship; he is a worship thief.

Worship creates a portal or a gate for the glory of the Lord to enter the earth realm, which allows for the transference of the keys to the gates of the region; the enemy cannot dwell in a region that offers up authentic worship to

Almighty God. There is a glory that God's people are getting ready to unlock. The glory is weighty, and if we worship, then the glory will come. When the new dimension of glory comes, we are going to be in awe; God is going to demonstrate whom He is! The enemy cannot stand the glory; that's what put him out of heaven. True worship comes from our spiritual knowledge of who God is, so we must know whom we worship.

A prophetic mind-set is imperative for acquiring the promises of God. In your journey as a believer, there will be an ongoing realization that what you want and need from God already exists in your "kingdom account" and that all you need to do is withdraw it from the supernatural and embody it in the natural realm. It is absolutely necessary to be able to foretell, confirm, and pronounce the promise of the vision. The prophetic word spoken cancels any other word spoken over the vision; it is necessary to keep making those declarations. It can be said that,

"The pronouncement of prophecy sets in motion a host of powers and events that can initially shake up a person's life before the word comes to pass. The shakeup happens so in its time what was spoken out of the mouth of the prophet can be materialized…Hindering forces, misguided ideas and beliefs, detrimental relationships or behaviors is challenged in the shakeup" (Price, 2008).

Chapter 6

The Brilliant Business Model

When God speaks to you, it is specifically to fulfill His will, which we know is good, acceptable, and perfect. We must understand the purpose of the vision that we receive from God. The manifestation is seldom instantaneous; it may take a while. A vision cannot be launched without spending hours, days, weeks, and sometimes even years in prayer. It is imperative to clearly understand the heart and mind of God, the creator of the vision, to ensure that it is properly tailored for the audience intended. It is essential to understand the needs of the people, the community, and the region. Whatever God has asked us or mandated us to do will fill a gap in the market, the Church, or the secular world. The instruction is based on meeting a specific need. We must offer an effective outcome to the vision to ensure that we remain competitive.

Communication inside and outside of the ministry or organization is essential. The correct alliances, what I term "holy alliances," are essential for where the body of Christ is going. Who we are connected to or intimate with will determine what we birth. The difficulty is discerning between long-term and short-term relationships. While it is important to build long-lasting relationships, we must also know who should be involved in the vision and how long that assignment is meant to last. As we know, relationships can aid or hinder the process of vision development. Communicating the vision and goals to all levels of the organism—the living, moving body of Christ, the Church—is essential if innovation is to take place. If a change occurs, it must occur at all levels. Innovation is a process through which people, systems, and organizations embrace the process of creative thinking to improve the quality, product, and service delivery of the organization (Derue and Rosso, 2012). Grace (2005) states that one of the characteristics of an organization that embraces innovation and change is its ability to determine the possibility for change; these possibilities may not always be obvious or indeed conventional. Leaders are required to think outside the norm, or what other organizations are already doing. The mind-set and attitude of the leadership team and the local church family also need to be developed to support innovation and change. The culture of the church and organization needs to be proactive as well as reactive. Potential problems need to be identified before they occur, and any problems that do occur must be addressed immediately.

Communication is also necessary to ensure that the transition process for those invested in the vision (and their families) is as smooth as possible. We need to recognize that many people do not respond very well to change; you will often hear people say, "We have always done it this way!" This phrase will keep us stuck in time. Some people will even try to hold the visionary hostage, meaning if the ministry is not centered on maintaining the status quo, these individuals may threaten to leave the ministry. We must understand that when God speaks, the provision has already been made to ensure that the vision does not fail, but that does not mean that the journey will be without its challenges. When God is about to do something, we must expect the adversary to try to oppose the move of God.

Diversification is another essential component in organizational culture. Ensuring that multiple needs are met at the same time, which may require several systems operating at the same time to ensure the success of the organization is essential. The organization needs to be able to change the product that they offer in order to meet the demands of the consumer and customer; the product is not the word of God. That is forever settled and unchanging; the product is how we reach people and how we deliver the word.

Speed is important to ensure an increased competitiveness and marketability; we have to be able to run with the vision. Society is changing rapidly, and we cannot afford to miss every opportunity presented to us to reach people. Sometimes we procrastinate because we cannot agree or we are fearful; we must hear God and move in time.

The organizational leader needs to consider decisions that will lead to changing its existing operations carefully to ensure that the organization is making the correct moves; decisions need to be based on sound, factual information and a discernment of the direction of the market in which the organization operates. The Apostle Paul was able to discern the hearts of the philosophers at Mars Hill in Acts 17:22 and address them based on where they were in their thinking. Decision-making is a complex process, which requires both innovation-based strategy and speed-based strategy.

The aim of the business model is twofold: to cultivate dedicated participants who see your vision as relevant and see that one of your goals is to build spiritual sons and daughters who commit themselves to walking with Christ and being loyal to the vision of the house in which God has planted them. The twenty-first century Church often struggles to understand the principle that the gospel never changes; God's Word is "yea" and "amen," forever settled in heaven. However, the application of the Word needs to change to meet the specific needs of the people and the era so that it can effectively carry the people into the perfect will of God.

Structural Contingency Theory (SCT)

A progressive and growing globalized marketplace requires organizations to embrace the change and creativity that lead to innovation practices; I want to examine this model in the context of the church. As living systems, the church will likely experience growth and development at specific times and seasons, requiring them to diversify their services and delivery to ensure survival. Innovation affects the values and culture of the organization, its various processes (such as goal setting), the stakeholders, communication, and the function of the church. As the Lord speaks to you, His instructions may be very different from what you have previously embraced as "doing church."

It is imperative that church develops a strong transition plan or even a backup plan to help guide them and their leaders through major changes. These plans should be well developed in order to ensure that the church, organizations, or businesses continue to remain effective in the marketplace. I have heard many times that the Church is dying and that it has become ineffective or irrelevant. That is not true and will never be the case. God has a plan for His bride, the Church, and we will tap into the plan of God concerning the Church and her relationship with the community.

It is essential for organizational leaders to be aware that internal and external environmental factors impact each other and could very well hinder the change process (Daft, 2010). Structural Contingency Theory (SCT) advocates that each organizational structure should be adaptable to each business and that each business must make moves to ensure they are operating within the most efficient structure to support the business; each organization should be a learning organization. Organizations must develop a capacity for innovation and an ability to react to new opportunities or unplanned threats. We are in the business of soul winning. If the Church is to survive, we must do the same.

Many scholars argue that a clear roadmap needs to be developed when implementing innovative changes. Each organization (or organism, as some say) needs to adopt a structured approach in terms of the principles and practices that it will use in this process. Depending on the nature of the organization and its goals, the principles and practices will vary. These components are complex, affecting all facets of the organization, and all relevant factors must be appropriately considered and addressed.

A systems approach in relation to change and innovation is important as it allows the visionary and his or her team to focus on the whole rather than just parts of the organization during the innovation process. With systems thinking, the relationship between the parts is the central focus of the change process. The models and theories that are used to create a structure for the innovation process provide a sound framework that supports change and provides the organization with the capacity to react to new opportunities or unplanned threats. Gone are the days when change could be implemented without conducting research, developing a sound plan, and putting support systems in place to ensure success and to allow the organizational members to feel safe. The elements, principles, and practices implemented to ensure the organization's success are all critical. With society experiencing so many changes and challenges, it is the opportune time for the Church to develop, let her voice be heard, and shine brightly in the midst of the darkness.

Internal Constraints and the External Environment

A number of factors referred to as contingency factors, influence the structural contingency decisions and plans of the organization. These factors can be identified in two main categories: internal influences and external influences. Leaders in successful, progressive organizations usually demonstrate behaviors of openness, creativity, self-efficacy, systematic thinking, and empathy. These leaders are able to examine past organizational performance as well as current performance and develop strategies for the future; it is so important for the Church to glean from such processes.

As we begin to shift into Apostolic Hubs sometimes known as Apostolic Centers or Spiritual Centers. C. Peter Wagner (2002) describes Apostolic Hubs as having four categories:

Name – It is a launching pad or a centrifugal.

Government – An apostle who mobilizes and equips the members for ministry and governs it. The elders support the apostle although the final authority rests with the apostle. The Holy Spirit delegates spiritual authority. The operation of the fivefold is an essential component of the governmental structure.

Focus – The focus is on the kingdom, influencing all areas of society, as opposed to being in the congregation. It is an agent of social transformation, making declarations, decrees, proclamations, and legislations in the realm of the spirit.

Operation – They fulfill the social expectation of a church in the areas of worship services, preaching, offerings, marriage counseling, funerals, childcare, youth ministry, care of sick and needy, weddings, and baptisms.

We need to identify our past successes and failures, how we have addressed social justice issues, and how we have we met the needs of our communities. In secular organizations, globalization has forced managers to rethink the structures of their organizations to ensure effectiveness. However, the Church needs to model effective change.

I have learned some fundamental lessons in this regard from the book of Nehemiah. Nehemiah was born in a period in which the presence of God was removed from the people, but his assignment was to bring consolation or comfort to the chosen people of God. I believe every leader has that God-given assignment. Nehemiah was an official, the king's cupbearer, too in the Persian court of King Artaxerxes I at the capital city of Shushan, which is now located near modern-day Iran. Nehemiah's countryman, Hanani (meaning "gracious") came and informed him concerning those who had escaped captivity and concerning the condition of Jerusalem. When Nehemiah received the report from his countryman, his *primary concern became*:

o   The Jews that had escaped from captivity Jerusalem

o   Remnant

o   Affliction

o   Reproach

o   Walls of Jerusalem were broken down.

o   Fathers' sepulchers (burying place and memorial) laid waste, the place where protection, order, and standards had been set.

o   The gates were burnt with fire

Nehemiah needed the favor of God in order to complete the assignment effectively, and he specifically prayed for this favor early in the journey. Nehemiah then implemented a seven-step process to ensure that he received a clear strategy for change. The Scriptures state that he…

1.   wept

2.   mourned

3.   fasted

4.   prayed

5.   reminded God of his covenant and mercy and of his promises to Moses

6.   confessed

7.   repented

Nehemiah prayed for four to five months, from Chislau (ninth month) to Nisan (first month). In his prayers, Nehemiah recognized that he needed the favor of both God and the king. If we can get to the king, we can appeal to his heart; an appeal to heaven is an appeal to the heart of God, but we must also appeal to the heart of man. By the time Nehemiah got into the presence of the king, the ruling authority, he knew what he wanted; in like manner, we must have a clear Word from the Lord before approaching earthly authorities. We have to open the heavens; the window of the favor of God must be on us. The favor of the Lord is better than money; it is like a master access key, and it will get us into places that we could not otherwise afford—places that our human rank or status alone would not allow us to enter. Nehemiah went to the king with a strategic plan, and the story played out as follows:

o   Nehemiah asked to be sent to his father's memorial so that he could build it and restore it to its former glory.

o   The king asked how long the journey would be. When would Nehemiah return?

o   Nehemiah received the blessing of the king.

o   The hand of God was good upon him.

○   Nehemiah set a timeline.

○   Nehemiah asked that letters be given to him for (1) credentials and protection (endorsed and mandated) and (2) resources.

○   The favor of the king was because of God. The king sent captains and horsemen with Nehemiah.

○   Nehemiah recognized that the place of promise had become a place of devastation.

○   Nehemiah was in Jerusalem for three days.

> Then said I unto them, Ye see the distress that we are in, how Jerusalem lieth waste, and the gates thereof are burned with fire: come, and let us build up the wall of Jerusalem, that we be no more a reproach. Then I told them of the hand of my God which was good upon me; as also the king's words that he had spoken unto me. And they said, Let us rise up and build. So they strengthened their hands for this good work. But when Sanballat the Horonite, and Tobiah the servant, the Ammonite, and Geshem the Arabian, heard it, they laughed us to scorn, and despised us, and said, What is this thing that ye do? will ye rebel against the king? Then answered I them, and said unto them, The God of heaven, he will prosper us; therefore we his servants will arise and build: but ye have no portion, nor right, nor memorial, in Jerusalem. (Nehemiah 2:17–20)

Nehemiah rose by night to view the condition of the city, and he did not tell anyone what God had put in his heart during the night season. We have to be able to see in the dark when it looks like there is no hope. The night was mentioned three times in chapter 2; in the night season, we see the condition of our situation, and God gives us the plan. When we approach governmental agencies and politicians, we must already have a workable plan. Nehemiah was able to assign the right families to build the different parts of the wall of Jerusalem, and he did not allow himself or those around him to succumb to the intimidation of the adversary. In Nehemiah 4:15–20, it said:

1. The enemy was infuriated and had great indignation against the Jews. In the midst of building, Nehemiah had some enemies that he had to be cognizant of—Sanballat the Horonite, Tobiah the servant, the Ammonite, and Geshem the Arabian. Everyone will not understand or support your vision.

2. The enemy mocked Nehemiah and the rest of the Jewish people with him.

3. The enemy spoke before the brethren and the army of Samaria to try and turn them against the Jews. Samaria means watch station—the compromising saints.

4. The enemy called the Jews feeble.

5. The enemy asked them what they were doing.

6. The enemy asked them if they would offer a sacrifice or giving offerings into and for the vision.

7. The enemy asked them if they would make an end in a day. In other words, is this task really achievable?

8. The enemy asked them if they would fortify or make themselves strong.

9. The enemy asked them if they would revive the stones out of the heap that is burned, or do you know what you are doing?

10. Tobiah indicated that even a fox would break down their wall; the vision would not have the lasting impact intended.

The questioning from the enemy was a process of intimidation, manipulation, and mind games. In Nehemiah 4:8, we see that the enemy "conspired all of them together to come and to fight against Jerusalem, and to hinder it." Nehemiah answered these adversaries in chapter 2, but he did not take the time to answer them in chapter 4 once the work was started; instead, he prayed, and the people continued to build. The walls were repaired and the breaches began to be stopped.

> And I sent messengers unto them, saying, I am doing a great work, so that I cannot come down: why should the work cease, whilst I leave it, and come down to you? (Nehemiah 4:3)

The enemy wanted to meet Nehemiah in the village of ONO, meaning "prolonged" or "strong." The enemy wanted to hinder success, ability, power, wealth, might, strength, force, and goods. We have to be cognizant of the mind control of the enemy. The Scriptures admonish us to gird up the loins of our mind:

> Wherefore gird up the loins of your mind, be sober, and hope to the end for the grace that is to be brought unto you at the revelation of Jesus Christ. (1 Peter 1:13)

We cannot move based on a counterfeit word; every word is not necessarily from the Lord:

> Afterward I came unto the house of Shemaiah the son of Delaiah the son of Mehetabeel, who was shut up; and he said, Let us meet together in the house of God, within the temple, and let us shut the doors of the temple: for they will come to slay thee; yea, in the night will they come to slay thee. And I said, Should such a man as I flee? and who is there, that, being as I am, would go into the temple to save his life? I will not go in. And, lo, I perceived that God had not sent him; but that he pronounced this prophecy against me: for Tobiah and Sanballat had hired him. Therefore was he hired, that I should be afraid, and do so, and sin, and that they might have matter for an evil report, that they might reproach me. My God, think thou upon Tobiah and Sanballat according to these their works, and on the prophetess Noadiah, and the rest of the prophets, that would have put me in fear. (Nehemiah 6:10–14)

In any organization, it is imperative that the internal structures are clearly defined: the organizational structure, tasks to be undertaken, communication systems, timelines, etc. We cannot afford to have any distractions. Nehemiah knew what structures were needed to fulfill the vision. He determined which families would build the wall, which families would build the gates, who would restore the temple and the other internal structures, what tools would be used, and the list goes on. The gates of the organization, the power of influence over the vision, the voices, must be secure so that these internal structures can be built. We cannot listen to any negative voices.

Nehemiah was concerned about the sepulchers of the fathers, the burying places, memorials, and graves. As visionaries, we must be concerned about the state of our nations, about what ideologies and belief systems are resurrected and buried. We cannot allow these memorials to lay waste and the gates that determine order and standards to be burned. We must be the gatekeepers of the nation and preserve the nation to be a place of protection, order, and standards.

Some scholars argue that five components need to be implemented while considering new products and services:

o   A strategy that will be employed to aid the innovation process

o   creative approaches to solving problems

o   the management of ideas

o   the processes of innovation that will be adopted

o   a suggestions system

This approach will ensure that the connectivity and interaction between the various parts of the organization and the environment will be appropriate and productive. Teamwork and "Cross-Functional Teamwork" members from all departments in the organization working together at all levels of the organization must take place. To reduce internal constraints, the organization must become a learning organization. The organization must become skilled in obtaining knowledge and translating that knowledge into best practices.

With change all around us, churches must now operate using SCT. The theory advocates the development of an alternative plan of organizational operation. SCT allows the analysis of change and the implementation process to focus on the whole of the organization and its partners rather than certain parts in isolation. Organizations must not engage in the change process without a plan or they may not achieve the change that they are hoping to achieve. As church and community leaders, we are now forced to examine the concerns of providing and measuring a quality spiritual and holistic experience for the body of Christ. The ability to be flexible and adapt to change is essential to the survival of any organization, and this process must be managed very carefully to facilitate organizational capacity for change, the organization's capacity for innovation, and the organization's ability to react to new opportunities or unplanned threats.

Innovation and Strategy

Innovation-based strategy fosters a culture that promotes the growth of the organization; these concepts can also be applied to a church environment. God is unfolding a strategic plan to shake, move, and shift the United States and perhaps other nations whose values systems have moved away from a biblical worldview. The role of leadership is critical—the leaders are the ones who will move the organization or church into change, communication, and collaboration. Vision and strategic planning are essential; the goals of the church need to be clear and achievable according to the will of God. The church also needs to be able to explore and develop the various options that will lead to success. This of the age church leaders is once again required to think outside the box and move beyond limitations, similar to the apostles of the early church and the pioneers of the Christian faith throughout each stage of the church age. Innovation is the result of creativity and change, and it can be described as the process, which leads a church to explore new dimensions of effectiveness. Leaders are able to ensure that all of the key players are invested in the process, whether through rewards, incentives, or consequences.

The strategic plan, the resources (technology, skill sets, etc.), and the necessary personnel must be specified in order to complete the desired task. A church's decision-making process is affected by the strategy that the church develops and adopts, and strategic drivers affect the strategic process.

Prayer is therefore essential to ensuring that all of the human and other resources needed to fulfill God's vision are supplied. The organization will then be able to diversify the products delivered to the customers when the needs arise. The culture adopted is an adhocracy culture, which is defined here:

> A dynamic, entrepreneurial, and creative place to work. Innovation and risk-taking are embraced by employees and leaders. Commitment to experimentation and thinking differently are what unify the organization. Long-term emphasis on growth and acquiring new resources. Success means gaining unique and new products or services. Being an industry leader is important. (Schoonmaker, 2006)

One of the characteristics of an organization that embraces innovation and change is its ability to determine the possibilities for change, especially when those possibilities are not obvious or conventional. Leaders are required to think outside the norm and beyond what other organizations are already doing. Improvisation is a significant component of innovation. The innovator is able to work on things that are not yet known and attach values to the factors revealed. Plans are then developed based on the factors and the values discovered. We must rely on the Spirit of God to lead us in this change process.

The organization needs to be conducive to change. It must be an organization that is readily able to adopt the mind-set that it is a living organism that will need to prepare for growth or even a metamorphic transformation. Grace (2005) argues that such organizations are able to "identify, hire, nurture, and stimulate" innovative individuals that will be an asset to their organization. Teams will be developed that will foster a culture of creativity. An environment must be created that will allow for learning, personal growth, and development.

During the building of the wall, the building of the gates, the restoration of the temple, and the restoration of true worship, Nehemiah surrounded himself with "God connections." Nehemiah's name means "consolation of Jah," and his father's name was Hachaliah, meaning "the darkness of Jah." Nehemiah was raised up in a season in which some of the children of Israel were in captivity, needing national identity and location. Consolation means to bring comfort in place of sorrow, disappointment, and grief.

We need to know the assignment in order to know who needs to be part of the team. One of Nehemiah's senior connections was Hanani, whose name means "gracious." Another significant team member was Ezra, whose name means "to aid or help." You need to have people who will speak life into the vision and not try to change the vision. When God gives you certain specifications, it is imperative to carefully follow every detail. Ezra was a scribe, and his job was to remind the people of the Word of the Lord. We all need an Ezra on the team. In chapter 8 of Nehemiah, Ezra read the law of God to the people, and I find it very interesting that he surrounded himself with leaders: six standing on his right side and seven standing on his left side. It is important to see who they were:

Men on the Left	Meaning	Men on the Right	Meaning
Pedaiah	Jah has Ransomed	Mattithiah	Gift of Jah
Mishael	Interposed - Becoming what God is	Shema	Announcement/ Sound
Malchiah	King of Jah	Anaiah	Jah has Answered
Hashum	Enriched	Urijah	Flame of Jah
Hashbadana	Considerate Judge	Hilkiah	Portion of Jah
Zechariah	Jah has Remembered	Maaseiah	Work of Jah
Meshullam	Allied		

Ezra had some powerful individuals standing with him. These individuals represented mindsets and concepts – how we need to think and speak. In the development of a God-given vision, it is essential to remember that it is the work of the Lord and that we are operating on behalf of the King. This is His portion, His work, and His gift to the Body of Christ and our communities. As visionaries, we merely interpose between the visions of heaven on earth.

The organization needs to be kept abreast of community needs, and it must know what it is willing to sacrifice in order to meet those needs. This is important if the organization wishes to remain competitive. Communication is imperative to determining the needs of the community. Building a long-lasting relationship with the community and the believers is also necessary for an innovative organization. Communication in terms of the impact of change on the saints will help ensure that the transition process is smooth.

Collaboration

According to Cardoso de Sousa, Pellissier, and Monteiro (2012), the role of leadership is critical; they are the ones that will lead the company into change, and communication, collaboration, and motivation are important. Cardoso de Sousa et al. posited that vision and planning are essential for innovation to be successful; the goals of the organization need to be clear and achievable. Cardoso de Sousa et al. argued that organizations should explore and develop the various options that lead to success. Denning and Dunham (2006) argue that the success rate of innovative ideas is very low: 4 percent actually. To enable innovation to succeed, it must be part of an ecosystem, an environment in which all the players interact and cooperate with each other. In the book of Ezra, all the different families came together as one man, the corporate man, to focus on the mission assigned:

> And when the seventh month was come, and the
> children of Israel were in the cities, the people gath-
> ered themselves together as one man to Jerusalem.
> (Ezra 3:1)

It is essential that the environment is not too restrictive, allowing a certain level of fluidity; remember, the gospel never changes, but the delivery and operation can be innovative. The changers and movers must possess the skills and experience to explore new methods. Innovation must be understood as an adoption of a new practice in which the participants need to the trained. Innovation then becomes a language that must be learned (Denning and Dunham, 2006). It is imperative that the participants speak the same language, with no misunderstandings, alterations, or deviations. Competence in the field is a requirement. Simply inventing new measures is inadequate when it comes to addressing problems; workable solutions must be identified. A correct definition of the problem will lead to an appropriate and correct solution. For the process to be successful, Denning and Dunham (2006) argue that there are several steps that need to be taken. These steps can be summarized as follows:

o   Exploring the possible problems.

o   Developing a new sense of reality.

o   Developing possible solutions.

o   Implementing an agreed upon plan.

o   Receiving new policies and procedures.

o   Creating an environment and culture that ensures the success of the new practices.

o   Leading with a belief that the plan is the best practice, with a genuine concern for all affected by the process.

The primary focus of innovation is that organizational resources such as people, tools, and ideas interact and work together. The process of innovation should arise when resources have not worked together effectively prior to that innovative process, and as a result, systems have been created to meet the needs of the organization or its customers. In the current global climate, individuals, groups, and organizations are required to reinvent themselves and think outside of the norm. Creativity and innovation have become synonymous terms, and they are expected of all kingdom movers and shakers.

Fact-finding and problem-solving should be natural skill sets for kingdom leaders. However, it is important to note that group work is an integral part of facilitating innovation and idea generation, and no one leader can do it alone. Group-level innovation leads to organizational innovation. The character of the organizational members will influence the overall character and structure of the organization.

Innovation is used in sociological, psychological, political, economic, and scientific senses, and it should also be used when pushing the kingdom of God into new dimensions and spheres of influence. Schumpeter (1934) first introduced the concept of innovation in terms of developing a new product for an existing or a new market. When addressing social problems, all aspects of innovation need to be explored. Innovation may make inroads into a new market or it may develop a new way of doing something. We must not allow stagnation and non-productivity to take place in the church; involvement in the local community is required. Collaboration and communication across aspects of the eco-system will also facilitate conflict resolution speedily when difficulties arise.

The Spirit of Originality

The Scriptures declare that we are fearfully and wonderfully made; we are unique, and we have a set of unique skills, gifts, and insights. I remember the Lord ministered to me a little while ago about the spirit of originality. When the Lord imparts a vision, it is often original, and many times, the original seems impossible. During this process, it is imperative to hear the voice of God clearly; one's mind needs to be clear and free of issues and concerns. Originality pulls upon our creative ability. Vision will birth the newness or freshness of an idea, a system, a method, or an operation. The spirit of originality has a twin called the spirit of the pioneer:

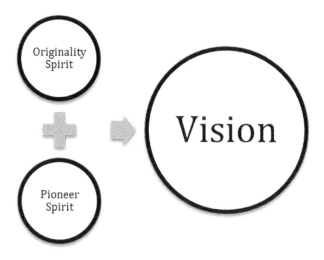

We have to remember that we came into the earth realm as originals. Originality means an ability to think or express oneself in an independent or creative manner. As the Lord positions us as leaders, we are releasing freshness in the earth. Sometimes, we may feel that the vision that we carry is not original; however, the location or delivery may be original. The spirit of originality or the spirit of the pioneer that the end-time leaders are walking in should reflect the spirit of creative power.

As I was meditating on vision, I began to relate the process of creation to a vision and the stages that the implementation of a vision may take. I find the Old Testament fascinating as it provides a typology of the New Testament and the Now Testament, the times we are living in now. The biblical worldview of creation is an excellent example of the developmental stages of vision. There are several schools of thought on the creation process; one of those schools of thought believes each day of creation was literal, while another school of thought believes that each day of creation was a time or geological periods. No matter what view we hold, as a creationist, I believe that God created by His word. We live in a word activated kingdom; God was able to bring order out of nothingness or chaos. Each stage of the vision is a time, and there is much to be learned from the creation process. The chart below provides a brief synopsis of the sequence of creation, the creation process, and my analysis of the vision process.

Sequence	Creation Process	Vision Process
Day 1	The heavens, the earth, light, and darkness	Bringing illumination to the dream of God.
Day 2	Heaven	Translating the things of the spirit, getting the idea into the earth realm and putting it on paper.
Day 3	Dry land, the seas, and vegetation	Identifying and prioritizing the mission of the vision.
Day 4	The sun, the moon, and the stars	Identifying the individuals associated with the vision.
Day 5	Living creatures in the water and birds in the air	Fleshing out the vision, in terms of the skills that the individuals will bring to the table.
Day 6	Land animals and people	Recognizing the inner circle that will bring the vision to pass and recognizing that you as the visionary are the pinnacle of the vision, in terms of ensuring that the dream comes to pass.
Day 7	God "rested"	Once the vision and all of its components are clear, it is now time to work the vision.

As we move in the realm of vision, we understand that we are making the invisible visible. Portals are sources of light, illumination, and blessing. A spiritual portal is the equivalent of all that the anointing can supply. It is a sign of God's approval and covenantal provisions. We must tap into the supernatural portals that transport and deliver creation's invisible products to the earth to be physically used by humanity. By nature and intent, spiritual goods were created for earth, and God set up portals in eternity as exit and entrance points to send them here. The Scriptures declare,

> The LORD shall open unto thee his good treasure, the heaven to give the rain unto thy land in his season, and to bless all the work of thine hand: and thou shalt lend unto many nations, and thou shalt not borrow. (Deuteronomy 28:12)

> The secret things belong unto the LORD our God: but those things, which are revealed, belong unto us and to our children forever, that we may do all the words of this law. (Deuteronomy 29:29)

> It is the glory of God to conceal a thing: but the honour of kings is to search out a matter. (Proverbs 25:2)

The Scriptures reveal that the Lord has a treasury, a storehouse of provision both in heaven and on earth. Covenantal blessings (promises and revelation) are providentially assigned and can be withheld for violation of God's Old Testament laws.

It is the will of God to bless the visionary and those connected with the vision; there will always be blessings associated with the vision. Blessings are designed to bring glory and honor to the Lord. God has promised that the blessings will unfold purpose in our lives. The blessings of the Lord have eternal purpose. It is imperative to remember the promises of God during the struggle of the formation of the vision. "And we know that all things work together for good to them that love God, to them who are the called according to his purpose" (Romans 8:28). The blessings are actually commendations from heaven (a eulogy) and God's final word on the matter (His benediction). The blessings are the consecrated gifts bestowed upon us by the Lord.

Sometimes, when it gets difficult during dark seasons and days of chaos, people may walk away. The Scripture is true: "The blessing of the LORD, it maketh rich, and he addeth no sorrow with it" (Proverbs 10:22). The Lord does not add sorrow, but sorrow may come when those who committed to walk with you or cover your back fall asleep on you and leave you exposed.

Birthing is a picture of breakthrough. Every birth is a miracle to the natural eye. As the psalmist said, babies are formed in secret (see Psalm 139:15). In this time in history, we have ultrasounds and three-dimensional imaging that will help us to have an idea of what the baby will look like but will not know the details until they arrive. We know that the baby is coming and that their coming creates both expectancy and great discomfort for the mother carrying the child. In the ninth month, the mother becomes desperate. It is as if nothing she does can bring her comfort. The pressure becomes intolerable. She is restless, uncomfortable, irritable, and without consolation. Only one thing will relieve her—the birthing of the baby. This is the same scenario for a vision, and when it comes to pass, it is a phenomenal feeling; what we bring into the earth realm is absolutely worth everything we go through.

I spent three years trying to change or tweak the vision because it was scary to others; we have to be true to the vision, the original vision that the Lord has given us. We must walk in the integrity of the vision. We cannot waste time doing that because God has a timeline for His will to come to pass in the earth. You have to keep those around you encouraged, but do not add to the vision or take away from the vision. Instead, identify the obstacles to the vision and then identify systems or strategies that you may need to put in place to ensure that the vision comes to pass.

Speak Life

We are in a word-activated kingdom (one that operates by faith), a "right now" kingdom. However, we are also in a kingdom where the seed must be "conceived," one that requires intimacy and time in order to bring forth fruit. We will experience seasons of hardship during the process of the vision. The gospels paint a beautiful picture of blessings associated with hardship. The book of Luke identifies four of the beatitudes given by Jesus during the Sermon on the Mount, which are listed below:

- ○   Blessed be ye poor: *for yours is the kingdom of God.*

- ○   Blessed are ye that hunger now: *for ye shall be filled.*

- ○   Blessed are ye that weep now: *for ye shall laugh.*

- ○   Blessed are ye, when men shall hate you, and when they shall separate you from their company, and shall reproach you, and cast out your name as evil, for the Son of man's sake. *Rejoice ye in that day, and leap for joy: for, behold, your reward is great in heaven: for in the like manner did their fathers unto the prophets.*

I declare that when you walk the vision out, you shall inherit the kingdom of God, you shall be filled and satisfied, you shall laugh again, and you shall leap for joy. The kingdom of God is God's governance in the earth realm (John 3:3–5). The kingdom of God must be sought: "But seek ye first the kingdom of God, and his righteousness; and all these things shall be added unto you" (Matthew 6:33).

We have access to the kingdom when we speak life and claim the following kingdom:

- ○   *Keys* —Matthew 16:19, "And I will give unto thee the keys of the kingdom of heaven: and whatsoever thou shalt bind on earth shall be bound in heaven: and whatsoever thou shalt loose on earth shall be loosed in heaven."

- ○   *Conversion, Childlike Faith, and Humility*—Matthew 18:3, "And said, Verily I say unto you, Except ye be converted, and become as little children, ye shall not enter into the kingdom of heaven."

- ○   *Selflessness* —John 5:20 "For the Father loveth the Son, and sheweth him all things that himself doeth: and he will shew him greater works than these, that ye may marvel."

These same principles are necessary in the development of vision: we have the keys or we are the key in the success of the vision, we must have childlike faith and humility to learn and grow, and finally, we have to be selfless during the process.

Chapter 7

Spiritual Activism

Spiritual activism is the activation of spiritual or kingdom ideas and concepts. Spiritual activism leads to acceleration of the promise, and the Church is required to actively engage in the discourse that is taking place in our nation over the role of the church in today's society. We must understand that there is a battle going on for the souls of humankind. The battle is over "mind-molders" that determine how we should think, which in turn will lead to how we should behave. In 1 Peter 1:13, it admonishes, "Wherefore gird up the loins of your mind, be sober, and hope to the end for the grace that is to be brought unto you at the revelation of Jesus Christ." The soul will be conscious in eternity; the book of Acts states that Jesus's soul would not be left in hell (Acts 2:31). The decisions we make during this war will affect us beyond our natural existence.

The Lord gave me a word in a dream I had in October of 2015: Murray's Law. I had never heard of this concept, but I learned that it has to do with the movement of living fluids in the body. A level of pressure is required for these fluids to continue to move within the veins or arteries. Living fluids have viscosity, so a pressure difference between ends of vessels is required for fluid to flow. The narrower the vessel, the more pressure is required to increase the volume flow rate, which translates to higher blood pressure when we have a hardening of the arteries. The Lord began to show me that America has suffered a hardening of a flow of love, kindness, vision, and productivity. Some areas and social structures of society no longer have the heart of God; there is no longer a free flow of the redeeming blood, the saving blood of Jesus through our nation, and respect and honor for almighty God. We have been consuming the wrong things, and that unhealthy diet has caused a hardening of the arteries.

The velocity of the flow of life is dependent on size, length, and blockages. The size represents the magnitude of the influence of the church in society, the length, the longevity and life of the influence and the blockages is the personal, and social and spiritual issues that may hinder the move of God. I believe that the implementation of a God-given vision, as well as the full operation of the fivefold ministry (the apostle, the prophet, the pastor, the evangelist, and the teacher) is the stent that will cause healing in our nation. The Lord is moving some visionaries and visions at an accelerated speed to ensure that our society continues to stand on a biblical foundation. Society is ready for change, and it needs what God has placed in us. The presence of healthy pressure is used to determine life, and as long as we feel the pressure that change is necessary, there is still life, and where there is life, there is hope. Force brings freshness and vigor; a change in the right direction is absolutely critical in this hour.

The Church is about to experience an acceleration of authority like never before. Acceleration can be described as the measure of the rate at which a defined amount of matter decreases or increases in velocity or speed; it is directly proportional to force. If mass remains constant, the acceleration will increase or decrease linearly with an increase or decrease in force. The Church has been experiencing a tremendous amount of pressure from the world to compromise her values and belief systems. The pressure is on, and we need to take a stand, sound the trumpet, call everyone and everything to attention, and bring back order in a world of chaos and impending anarchy.

We are in a season of faster or greater activity, development, progress, and advancement. There is a sense of urgency to restore godly and kingdom principles and systems; there is certainly no time to waste. We must catch the vision and prepare for the transition; we must teach the vision to those around us and be steadfast and firm concerning what the Lord has told us. There has to be a paradigm shift (paradigms belong to the realm of concept, and then they birth structure). We have to be in alignment with heaven and with the vision of the house. We are going back to the original plan of God: *the Eden mandate*. The fivefold Eden anointing is being restored to the body of Christ:

1. fruitful

2. multiply

3. replenish

4. subdue

5. dominion

Genesis 1:27–28 lets us know that we have been created in the image and likeness of our Creator. We have to know our spiritual DNA and the heritage that the Lord of heaven bestowed upon us from the beginning. Be fruitful and multiply and replenish the earth and subdue it and have dominion. We have some awesome leaders in the Bible that made a significant difference in their respective contexts:

1. *Abraham* – dealt with self and family to prepare to be a nation

2. *Moses* – dealt with Pharaoh and delivered a nation

3. *Joseph* – spoke the vision of the Lord into the atmosphere, positioned his heart to walk uprightly before God and man, and served in whatever capacity the Lord allowed him to be in with grace, humility, integrity, love, and forgiveness

4. *Nehemiah* – rebuilt a city, reorganized a people, and reinstituted worship

5. *Jonah* – brought a nation to repentance

6. *The apostles* – turned the world upside down (Acts 17:6). They challenged the political systems inadvertently by preaching the gospel.

Christianity needs to become the nation's standard again! As leaders, our assignment is to bring order out of chaos, and we must be convinced in our hearts that one person can make an incredible difference. As leaders, I suggest that we need to know that it is:

- Time to determine the kingdom agenda.

- Then it's time to develop a prayer center, win souls, and bring order back to our nation.

- God will never give you anything you can't handle; every vision from God is bigger than you, and it is going to take great faith.

- The passive bride must arise to submit to and follow the groom.

- Impartation of focus – We can be what we have seen.

- We must receive a grace that will empower us to negotiate the will of God in different sectors.

God is releasing an anointing, and the Scriptures declare, "And it shall come to pass in that day, that his burden shall be taken away from off thy shoulder, and his yoke from off thy neck, and the yoke shall be destroyed because of the anointing" (Isaiah 10:27). I heard the Lord say the following to the end-time believers:

- You are a seat of influence; protect the DNA of God.

- You have a champion's anointing and mantle; there will be a release of the apostolic mantle to possess and occupy (advance the kingdom of God and push back the kingdom of darkness).

- Know your Word, and know what you are going to bring to the table; study to show yourself approved of God and man.

- What is your mandate? You must know and move in your assignment with discipline and a controlled appetite.

- You must have a finisher's anointing; no more procrastination or stopping part of the way through the assignment.

- You must walk in a new level of humility.

The gates of hell shall never prevail against the church (Matthew 16:18); we have been set up for success. Even under pressure, the church will bring forth life. When heaven and earth kiss, there is life, and we kiss heaven with our worship and intercession. In the Scriptures, the body of the prophet brought life to that which was dead:

> And Elisha died, and they buried him. And the bands of the Moabites invaded the land at the coming in of the year. And it came to pass, as they were burying a man, that, behold, they spied a band of men; and they cast the man into the sepulchre of Elisha: and when the man was let down, and touched the bones of Elisha, he revived, and stood up on his feet. (2 Kings 13:20–21)

This type of anointing will break through every obstacle and hindrance to the implementation of the vision. It will shake every shackle loose that attempts to keep the vision and the visionary from coming into fullness. Jesus promises that "the Kingdom suffers violence and the violent take it by force." The breakers anointing should be the core anointing of the church for the purpose of advancement. One of the names of God is the Breakers anointing as we can see in Micah 2:13 "The breaker is come up before them: they have broken up, and have passed through the gate, and are gone out by it: and their king shall pass before them, and the LORD on the head of them." The breakers anointing opens the gates of heaven to allowing heavens resources into the earth realm. Austin (2003) states, "When the breaker anointing occupies an area, individuals, churches, socio-political structures, and belief systems are revolutionized. The Breaker must come if we are to see the transformation of our cities."

Capacity for Change

In the process of developing a vision, an organization will likely need to reorganize itself; change is necessary to facilitate the increased capacity that the vision demands. Change is a difficult concept or process, and it is not easy for individuals or corporations to step outside of the norm into a place of faith. Sometimes, the current organizational structure will not facilitate the vision, and readiness for change is one of the most influential factors that affect the design of the change process. It is imperative that the leader takes the time to ensure proper planning. A useful tool for analyzing the need for change is called the Root Cause Analysis (RCA) model.

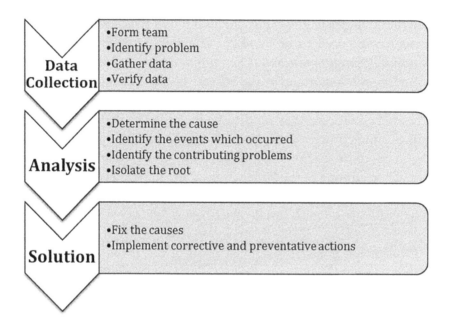

Readiness for change is one of the most influential factors that affect the design of change. Proper planning needs to occur. A useful tool to use when analyzing the need for change is the use of Root Cause Analysis (RCA). It recognizes that no organization has a 100 percent success rate in all the projects that they may undertake. RCA is the process undertaken to prevent a problem from reoccurring or to identify the need for change within an organization. A clear plan of intervention, a clear diagnosis of the problem, is critical to the success of the intervention. This will facilitate the organization's willingness to change.

The goal of every organization is to ensure that the process is on-going. This model helps to minimize the problems that a church may face in project development or the need to change a system for the church to survive, particularly in a globalized economy where the potential dynamics has been expanded. To reduce the errors, it is imperative to identify where the system is weak. It is essential to know why adverse events have occurred as well as what happened and how it happened. Once the cause of the problem is understood, then corrective action can be taken. The plan needs to be supported by the appropriate knowledge. Skills, church structure, people, and resources all need to be in place. The ability of the leadership to motivate change is essential. The training of the leadership as agents of change is important to the success of the strategic plan. There must also be tools or benchmarks in place to measure the success of the change process; they need to be identified or developed during the planning process. Example tools are participant's surveys or feedback, compliance reports, proficiency measures or matrices, etc.

The attitude of the leader could affect the success of the implementation of change. Dalziel and Schoonover (1988) identify three types of leaders, which can be described as follows:

- Visionary leaders – They see change as necessary due to changes occurring around them.

- Technocratic leaders – They focus on the outcome of change and pay very little attention to the individuals affected by the process.

- Sympathetic leaders – Their focus on the individuals affected by the change is detrimental to the overall success of the implementation of change.

For the successful implementation of change, it is imperative to identify the opportunities and threats to the change process. For example, in the case of a ministry, the goal of the ministry should be to increase productivity in the church population and to improve the use of resources. To this end, it is essential for the ministry to focus on the following:

- The mission.

- Innovative and creative processes.

○ Realistic and reliable solutions to problems identified.

○ The appropriate skills and anointing to implement the plan of God.

○ The kingdom accountability requirements. Kingdom accountability is ensuring that the vision lines up with the word of God and that the vision is kingdom-focused, not the focus of a personal agenda.

○ The needs of the ministry, the members, the community, etc.

Trust

Trust is also a very important factor to consider, for the achievement of stated goals can only be "made possible by the company's trust-based corporate culture" (Galan, et al, 2009, 61). Trust requires that you put your faith, confidence or hope in a person, process or system. Trust will lead you to believe in and support the vision and the visionary. Hebrew 10:35 encourages us to "Cast not away therefore your confidence, which hath great recompense of reward." We must know when God speaks, rest in it. The spoken word will bring an exceeding reward, a recompense of what was sacrificed in the process of bring the vision to pass, whether it was time, resources, relationships, strength or hope. Hebrews 11:1 declares that, "Now faith is the substance of things hoped for, the evidence of things not seen." A substance can be defined as confidence. Confidence in the word of God will yield productivity; it will allow the invisible to become visible. I have leaned over time that speaking the work of God over his promise is like watering a seed planted in good soil when exposed to the correct elements, the right atmosphere it will be productive. Trust eventually produces life. There is a distinct difference between trust and arrogance, we cannot be self-reliant, self-important, be conceited or have an exaggerated opinion of our self or what we think; we must surround our self and the vision with wise counsel and wait patiently on the process, knowing that God is in control.

Trust needs to be built with the stakeholders, including church leaders, lay members, and the community. The visionary needs to ensure that all the stakeholders are committed to change, that the ministry has the ability to succeed, that the resources provided are adequate, that the relevant policies and procedures are in place, and that the change process will be amended when appropriate. This is especially important during the death of the vision; most visions experience a season of death, where it appears that the vision will not come to pass; it is a biblical principle, even in nature death proceeds life, winter proceeds spring. The vision may start off great, then hits a plateau or even dies; but eventually, it is resurrected with new life, stronger and more powerful. There may be times where everyone may not see or support the vision. It is imperative to speak life and understand that everyone does not see the same things at the same time and that people are allowed to ask questions. We have what we speak, speak a harmonious team into existence. If we treat people negatively that is how they will react.

We must understand that stakeholders should incorporate community leaders as well. The vision is not just about the self-preservation of the church but about the growth and expansion of the church, the organization, or the organism. The church must gain enough respect to be the moral voice or moral compass of the community.

Cultural Context

Morgan-Scott (2013) argues that there is six attributes that an organization should have in order to be ready to implement change:

- The organization must have a clear understanding of its history of change.

- The organization needs to clarify the expectations of change, and those expectations need to be shared with all levels of the organization.

- The organization needs to own its problems or concerns, as well as its ideas and thoughts about how the change will resolve the issues.

○   Top-level management needs to support the change process.

○   The plan needs to be compatible with the organizational goals.

○   The cultural context in which change takes place is essential to the success of the change process. The research needs to ensure that those who are making the changes are familiar with the organization's current culture.

The visionary becomes the change agent, and the change agent must be aware of his or her capabilities with regard to implementing change at a particular location, time, or environment. This understanding will greatly affect the design of the change required. A change agent may design change based on his or her capabilities, his or her personality, or the cultural norms and values of the organization. The climate will need to support the change process. A climate of worship, intercession, sacrifice, and commitment to the vision needs to be created.

When God speaks, change is required. Visions that only the leaders see are insufficient for ministry movement. Leaders must inspire others to see the exciting future possibilities of a new vision. Communicating a vision is then an act of persuasion; the visionary must convince the stakeholders that the vision is right for the time and right for the ministry.

The visionary must build the church community. Whitehead and Whitehead (1991) argue, "A community is a gathering of people who supports one another's performance…community is a place where we learn to hold one another." A church community must cultivate and operate in an eightfold anointing:

1.   Wholeness incorporating diversity.

2.   A shared culture; a "buy in" to the vision.

3.   Good internal communication among the leadership and the entire body of Christ.

4.   Care, trust, and teamwork.

5.   Group maintenance and a solid governmental structure.

6. Delegated leadership—the visionary should not carry the entire weight of the ministry alone but should make time for prayer and study the Word of God.

7. The development of young people; helping them cultivate a love for God and preparing them for leadership.

8. Links with the outside world.

Transformational Leadership

The concept of transformational leadership can be very useful for the visionary. Transformational leadership is a process adopted by a leader along with their team to identify a necessary change in the church. Morgan-Scott (2013) argues transformational leadership as the process by which change occurs through the power and authority exercised by an individual or group of individuals. Transformational leadership is the process by which structural transformation occurs within the organization. Organizational improvement and organizational effectiveness are the primary goals of transformational leadership. Leaders may be transformational in character and ability. Transformational leadership also aims to ensure that the change process addresses forms of discrimination such as racism, sexism, etc. Discrimination can be a concern in the body of Christ because, at times, we are a reflection of our society. We cannot operate effectively in the midst of division, and we need each gift to operate effectively. This style of leadership provides a deeper form of change, as well as a more equitable form of change. Transformational leadership recognizes that change is often hindered by deeply rooted (and often unconscious) biases in individuals and organizations.

Transformational leadership promotes a particular process that leaders and saints may adopt in achieving ministry goals. "Transformative leadership is an exercise of power and authority that begins with questions of justice, democracy, and the dialectic between individual accountability and social responsibility" (Weiner, 2003, 89). It is a process in which structural transformation occurs within the organization. Organizational improvement and organizational effectiveness are the primary end goals; this includes reaching our communities. Shields (2009) believes that organizational improvement can only be achieved through a focus on four factors:

- Setting direction
- Developing people
- Redesigning the organization
- Managing the training or staff development program

Transformational leadership leads to collective engagement in the attempt to achieve a common goal. The performance of groups is central to the overall performance of the ministry. Innovation and creativity are imperative in order for the ministry to maintain the competitive edge that leads to longevity. Let me be clear: having a competitive edge does not mean that you have to compromise the doctrine of Christ or the principles of the Word of God!

Servant-Leadership

We have to be both leaders and servants. The first mention of the word "servant" in the Bible is in Genesis 9:25: "And he said, Cursed be Canaan; a servant of servants shall he be unto his brethren." This simply means that you are submitted under the authority of another, in servitude to them. When developing a vision, we have to be careful not to become what I call a "serpent-leader." We cannot be wise in our own understanding; instead, we must seek the heart, the mind, and the will of God. In the world of business, it has become too easy to be unscrupulous, evil, deceptive, presumptuous, treacherous, manipulative, vengeful, and vindictive. Obviously, all of these characteristics do not represent Christ. The lies and deception of the serpent create false thoughts and perceptions in people. The characteristics of Satan are abominable, and there is no good thing in him: "He was a murderer from the beginning, and abode not in the truth, because there is no truth in him. When he speaketh a lie, he speaketh of his own: for he is a liar, and the father of it" (John 8:44).

We have to be careful when leading others that we do not become venomous snakes who often deliver deadly defensive or even offensive bites without warning. This can especially happen when we are frustrated with the process or when we subject ourselves to serpent-leaders on our team. Jesus said, "Behold, I give unto you power to tread on serpents and scorpions, and over all the power of the enemy: and nothing shall by any means hurt you" (Luke 10:19).

Servant-leadership is a specific leadership practice and set of leadership philosophies. Traditional leadership generally is the accumulation and exercise of power by one person at the "top of the pyramid." By comparison, the servant-leader shares power, tasks, and responsibilities puts the needs of others first, and helps people develop and perform as highly as possible. "But it shall not be so among you: but whosoever will be great among you, let him be your minister; And whosoever will be chief among you, let him be your servant: Even as the Son of man came not to be ministered unto, but to minister, and to give his life a ransom for many" (Matthew 20:26–28). Servant-leadership often does not come with glory and honor, but we need to know that we are free in Christ: "For he that is called in the Lord, being a servant, is the Lord's freeman: likewise also he that is called, being free, is Christ's servant" (1 Corinthians 7:22). It is incredibly liberating to be in the perfect will of God fulfilling your assignment. Our ultimate goal is to ensure that society is built up and that the biblical worldview is the central focus of our living and decision-making.

Moral Code

It is imperative that every leader and every ministry has a moral code of personal and organizational operation and engagement with others. Morgan-Scott (2013) indicates that it is essential to understand the necessity of the following:

- The code of ethics significantly impacts the ministry culture and ethical behavior within the organization/ organism.

- O   The code of ethics is essential to the successful operation of any organization/organism, particularly in terms of the protection of both the environment and the rights of individuals.

- O   In the current global climate, ethical behavior is a serious concern, and the code of ethics is a must-have for all organizations/organisms.

- O   A corporate code of ethics sets the expected standard of behavior for those in the organization/organism, and it allows those outside of the organization/organism to know what to expect, as well.

- O   Some codes of ethics also provide consequences for inappropriate behavior and provide guidance for a complaint process; we need a disciplinary structure in the Church as well as in the corporate world.

The code of ethics defines the standards for acceptable behavior among a ministry's leaders; integrity is essential in all stages of vision implementation. An ethical culture helps to ensure that both the leaders are committed to providing a competent and true worship experience, one that can be trusted. In my experience, the code of ethics communicates the morals and values in a clear manner for all to understand. The code of ethics can sometimes be translated into a code of conduct. It is often a statement of commitment and competency on the part of the ministry, and it provides expectations for the consumer during business transactions, in the development of the worship experience, and in terms of how people will be treated. The purpose of the code of ethics is fivefold and can be defined by what I call "The Power Rs":

- O   *Righteousness* – This is a central component as it develops a basis of trust between the ministry and the saints. The character of the organism and its members are of paramount importance. Righteousness and integrity build on characteristics such as honesty, trust, etc. Integrity promotes transparency and openness in the ministry.

○ *Revelation* – The goals and vision of the ministry need to be communicated and perpetuated throughout the organism. Communication reinforces the standards that the leaders will adhere to, leaving the members with no ambiguity of expectations. Communication also provides a forum for the purposes of accountability.

○ *Roles and Responsibilities* – The role that each player should adopt to ensure his or her success and the success of the overall vision is defined through this area.

○ *Risk* – The code of ethics attempts to minimize adverse risks that the ministry may face, as well as risks that the visitor may take in the worship and deliverance process.

○ *Reputation* – Reputation is vital to the present and future survival of any ministry. The code of ethics, whether written or verbal, attempts to build and keep the good reputation or refute the poor reputation of the ministry and its worship service.

There must be a set standard of operation in the church to facilitate those who come for worship, deliverance, and healing. God is a God of principle, and He will not come in uninvited; neither will He come into a polluted atmosphere. We must remember that Jesus is the center of it all.

Chapter 8

A Working Model

Vision Model

The implementation of vision is incredibly important. For example, the vision of our church, Shiloh Worship Center, is to bring people to a place of rest, abundance, and peace in their spirits, souls, and bodies so that they can experience a fulfilled life through Jesus Christ. This is an exciting time for the body of Christ, as we continue to covenant with God for revival, a returning of people to Christ. We recognize that people are hungry for the truth and want to be in the presence of the Lord, for in His presence is fullness of joy; at His right hand there are pleasures forevermore (Psalm 16:11). In the Scriptures, Shiloh was the place where the tabernacle of the Lord was set up (read Joshua 18:1). We created a culture that each member of our family that would partake of this God-ordained ministry, would have an encounter with Jesus Christ that would be transformational, life changing. Our worship experience allowed God's presence is in our midst. In every season, we should be pushing forward the kingdom agenda; we believe the love of Christ must permeate every stratum and sphere of our communities.

In your experience at Shiloh, you will find *rest*. For so long, the enemy has been seeking to destroy us and steal our destinies in the Lord. You will discover that when you surrender all to God, you will rest from the labor of this life and come to know that God has everything under control (Hebrews 4:10–11). The exciting part is that you will begin to enjoy your earthly existence and experience a refreshing renewal in your life.

As we move toward *abundance*, your life will not be the same again. You will abound in grace, faith, morality, hope, joy, righteousness, thanksgiving, truth, wisdom, knowledge, understanding, spiritual gifts, ministry, power, physical health, and material benefits— complete deliverance in every area of your life. Jesus declared, "I have come that you might have life, and have it more abundantly" (John 10:10). The anointing of the Lord is able to minister to the needs of the meek, heal the brokenhearted, liberate those held captive to the cares of life and to the enemy, and open the prison doors for those who are bound spiritually, mentally, emotionally, or physically (Isaiah 60:1–2). It is time for us to live like the children of the King and access our kingdom privileges through Christ.

Finally, you will find *peace*. There will be a harmonious relationship between you and God that will come through the Word (Acts 10:36). Reconciliation with God will bring a sense of wholeness, contentment, and freedom that cannot be experienced outside of an intimate relationship with Him. You will then begin to develop the characteristics of Jesus Christ, which is our ultimate aim.

Shiloh has come, and there is *rest*, *abundance*, and *peace*! Here at Shiloh, it's a RAP! There is no chaos, lack, or unrest!

Our vision was developed in such a way that all age groups could relate to it. We felt it necessary to engage the young people in particular to ensure that we pass the legacy of a righteous church, a church in good standing with God, to them. The core values and the culture that we adhere to include values such as love, dedication, integrity, faithfulness to God and others, respect, faith, purity, holiness, unity, building (as opposed to destroying), making a difference, providing, preaching, and knowing and sharing. Every house has a culture, and it is essential to know that culture in order to perfect it and maintain it.

Strategic Plan

After the corporate vision has been established, it is important to develop a strategic plan. In our strategic plan, we determined that we are in the era of the resurrection of the corporate man, a unified team of individuals or departments working together collaboratively. With the application of the kingdom blueprint, we can fulfill and maintain the kingdom agenda. The kingdom mandate can be described as the plan of God for the earth realm. "Thy kingdom come. Thy will be done in earth, as it is in heaven" (Matthew 6:10), and more specifically for your project. We must identify, strategically pursue, and consistently maintain the kingdom agenda in our region. The Church is the ruling authority in the earth realm.

We have clearly expressed that we have dedicated our lives to the ministry of Jesus Christ, "for in him we live, and move and have our very being" (Acts 17:28). This is a ministry of excellence, and we recognize that we are servants of the Lord ministering to the Lord and to His great people (1 Kings 3:9). For many reasons, some individuals have been living below God's expectations for their lives; there is no time to live as defeated people. This is especially true in this season. Through the power of the Holy Spirit, we will transform the lives of those around us for generations to come.

The strategic plan has multiple dimensions which…

1. Will be a blueprint that will provide a detailed framework and principles that will move the church toward her destiny over the next twenty years.

2. Establish the Word of God as the principle guide for the character and culture of the ministry.

3. Establish the growth of the ministry over the next twenty years, developing the ministry for the next generation.

4. Provide focus to the direction that the ministry will take in the next five years.

5. Establish the importance of growth, both in numbers and impact within the community.

6. Enhance the spiritual growth and development opportunities of both the corporate man and each individual member.

7. Ensure economic growth and financial responsibility.

The plan must then be developed, explicitly outlining how the mission is going to be implemented. A business plan is also needed if the project is trying to attract funding. In terms of the superstructure, the mission should determine how the needs of those in the organism and organization are going to be met. Then, in terms of the corporate structure, the mission should also determine how the needs of those outside of the organism or organization (the community) are going to be met.

In the plan, we establish our local, regional, national, and international reach. One can argue that globalization is a significant concern in terms of the state of the world's economy. The term *globalization* has become popular over the past few years as the nature of the world economics and interactions has changed, along with changes in politics, social culture, and technology. Local, regional, and international variable impact each other, which is reflected in bilateral relationships, multilateral relationships, and regional agreements.

> The essence of the process of globalization is represented in the ease of movement of people, information and goods between the countries on a global scale, and the effect of this on economic relations in general and the North and South dialogue in particular. (Al-Katatsheh and Al-Rawashdeh, 2011, 108)

We are now in the era of a globalized economy, where there is an integration of wealth, capital goods, technology, jobs, etc. Many industrialized nations, particularly those in the TRIAD, Western Europe, Asia, and the North America are investing in countries that can produce goods at a low cost, provide labor at a low cost, and can aid the investor to gain a constant flow of capital. Goods trading and foreign investment has grown over the past few years.

Some scholars argue that the conflicts and contradictions within globalization are necessary for the survival of the world economy. Al-Katatsheh and Al-Rawashdeh (2011) states that globalization is primarily focused in reducing the gap between the north and the south in terms of wealth and social justice, ensuring that the needs of the people in which the global free-market is exercised and met.

The economy of the church must be far reaching across denominational boundaries and organizations barriers to ensure effectiveness in our communities. An effective leader is required to adapt to the changing economic structure. This means change in every area of the organization, to include both macro- and micro-level changes regarding how the church responds to internal and external forces. Collaborations and alliances can yield enormous benefits in the exchange of ideas and resources. "Globalization is an incontestable reality of our days and has major implications upon the world market system of relations and even upon our destiny of each national component" (Mangra, Stanciu, and Mangra, 2009, 85). I have found that visuals and diagrams are an excellent way to help team members and others understand this reality.

Shiloh's strategic plan is detailed enough that anyone can pick it up and run with it. A prophetic mind-set in this instance means that, we believe that the invisible, the word or the promise, will eventually come to pass or manifest into reality in the right time. "And the LORD answered me, and said, Write the vision, and make it plain upon tables, that he may run that readeth it. For the vision is yet for an appointed time, but at the end it shall speak, and not lie: though it tarry, wait for it; because it will surely come, it will not tarry. Behold, his soul which is lifted up is not upright in him: but the just shall live by his faith" (Habakkuk 2:2–4). You may not be able to accomplish all areas of the plan immediately; it will require that you know what God has called you to do, that you set timelines, and that you have much faith.

Vision Emergence Template (VET)

As I began to study and seek the Lord about how to develop the vision, the Lord downloaded a model to me. In the model development, three key components were necessary to identify: the sections to be covered, the objectives for each section, and the project details that would ensure the success of each objective. It is critical that the planning team develops agreed upon timelines for each project objective. A completed version of the model can be seen below, and appendix 2 provides a blank template for your use.

Sections	Objectives	Project Details
Project Coordinator **Project Consultant**	Identifies the overview of the project. Team leader who will keep the project on task. Provides technical support.	This person will birth the vision. Will provide a framework for the vision, such as site plans, will edit the proposal for the vision
Introduction 1. Concept 2. Philosophy 3. Overview	How and why the vision was birthed. Discuss the importance of the vision. Provide an overview of how the vision will be executed.	Provide a brief description of the history and mission of the ministry. Why is there a need or a demand for the vision? The ideology behind the vision. The mission of the vision and its expected outcomes.
Mapping Geographical Location	Justification of the project in the particular region.	Provide statistical information such as social groups, unemployment, etc. Information from the Metropolitan Statistical Area (MSA) and your local Chamber of Commerce.
Job Creation	Justify the need for support for the pending project.	How will the project be beneficial for the economy?

Reaching into the Future	What kind of legacy will the project leave for the generations to come?	Use the county Needs Assessment report. Visit with your local and neighboring city council managers, the mayor, the economic development department, and your district representative.
Project Uniqueness	Appeal to the hearts of the investors to convince them to engage in an innovative and creative project.	How the project will heal or enhance the community. Be explicit about what the project will offer. For example (5 years): conference center college prep program walking trail research center
Qualities of the Leadership Team	To reassure the investors and the community that the project is legitimate.	Identify each project team member and provide a brief biography.
Entrepreneurial Investment	Build a network of individuals that will support the project financially, emotionally, and through all necessary resources.	Be explicit about what you need and how it will be used.
Stakeholders	Identify all who will be involved in the project.	Example (2–3 months): church city council district representative

Partners, Helpers, and Donors	State what kind of investors you are looking for, how much you are requesting, and for how long.	Grants or donations, example additional statement: "An investment in this project is an investment in future generations."
Project Goals 1	What does the project hope to achieve, and what are the timelines?	Example (5 years): Build a research center to both educate the community and support the local schools in the fields of science, technology, engineering, and math.
Project Goals 2	What does the project hope to achieve, and what are the timelines?	Example (10 years): Build sustainable housing to address the sustainable energy issues.
Project Goals 3	What does the project hope to achieve, and what are the timelines?	Example (3 years): Build a day care promoting a biblical worldview that will raise Christ-centered children.
Other Important Components	Capture the attention of the reader	• Innovative project name • Branding—logo • Every page needs to be bright and colorful • Site map • Photographs • Renderings

Project Coordinator

The project coordinator should always be either the visionary or someone whom the visionary trusts to ensure that the project is carried out to the required specifications. A brief biography of the visionary should be placed in this section, even if that person will not be undertaking the day-to-day tasks of coordinating the project. The biography should be structured in such a way that the readers and possible project investors will be confident that the project coordinator is qualified, committed to the vision, and capable of the task. This section should give the readers a desire and an enthusiasm to read the rest of the brochure or document. Sell, sell, sell; no project or visionary can stand on its own. Remember, what the Lord has given you is for the community, and someone somewhere has been waiting for the emergence of the vision.

This section must also provide an overview of the project. Individuals involved in the project often get excited and sometimes want to add to or take away from the vision in the name of making improvements. I am not saying that the vision cannot be fluid, but changes should only be made as a result of much prayer, wisdom, and advice; be firm and confident in what the Lord has given you, even if others do not see it.

Project Consultant

To bring credibility to the project, it is imperative to seek the wisdom of someone who is an expert in the field. For example, I am a pastor and an educator, but I have never built houses; if I were an investor, I would be nervous about giving my hard-earned cash to someone who has no experience. The project coordinator will provide a framework for the vision, which may include site plans, an edited proposal for the vision, and expertise along each step of the journey. Shiloh's project consultant is a very experienced architect who has worked in his field for over forty years on various projects for the city and private companies.

Introduction

The introduction is tridimensional: philosophy, concept, and overview. For this section, it is essential to conduct some research. I used sources like the local Chamber of Commerce, local and national newspaper articles, and data from the Center on Budget and Policy Priorities. In this section, I shared how the investment group was birthed, its function in the project, and its particular focus. I also outlined the mission of the vision and its expected outcomes. You must identify what the project offers the community, why it is essential, why it will be successful, and the legacy that it will leave behind. It is imperative to explain how the project is undergirded. I want to share with you the introduction that I developed for the Intelligence Village project:

Intelligence Village (Intelliville)

Established in 2011, the Shiloh Family Investment Group (F.I.G.), a DBA of Shiloh Worship Center International, is excited to announce the development of the Intelligence Village (Intelliville) community. Shiloh F.I.G. is a unique investment group, which offers an innovative approach to technological research and the nurturing of analytical and creative thinkers who will have the ability to contribute to the potential education development in the market rather than react to market forces. Secondly, we focus on building character, leadership traits, and the moral-ideological thinking of future generations through the creation of community resources, which will impact our region, our nation, and the global market. Thirdly, Shiloh F.I.G. will respond to economic and housing development needs locally, nationally, and internationally. The vision of Shiloh F.I.G. is also to develop foresight in terms of other investment needs as determined by the group. We gain clarity and sharpness of vision to move strategically toward the mission ahead of us through analyzing, understanding, gaining knowledge and wisdom of globalization, recognizing market forces, and recognizing the current movements of the global market, which allow us to identify the potential needs of the market in the future.

The Intelliville community will be a culture and knowledge development center. The research center aims to stretch the thinking and challenge the perspectives of the residents. The concept of an intelligence village is a community of excellence, which is designed to focus and stimulate the talents, capabilities, and gifts of those living in the community. This, in turn, will lead to the exploration of the depth and potential of the human heart and mind. The unique exposure to like and unlike, and the concentration of human talent coupled with competition and collaboration, produces greater art, science, technology, and business. The community will promote the solutions to key problems that humanity faces in the areas of technology, economics, science, etc. The underlying philosophical concept and culture of the community will be fourfold:

1. The community will promote Christian values, which will underpin organizational structures, operational procedures, learning, and development.

2. The research institute will be established with a heavy emphasis on creativity and innovation.

3. The community will implement a strong academic curriculum in science, technology, engineering, and math (STEM).

4. The schools located on site will benefit from the skills of the staff of the research institute.

In the Bible, the word "intelligence" was first mentioned in Daniel 11:30. The Hebrew word for intelligence is "biyn", which means to separate mentally, or distinguish one group of individuals from another; the root meaning of the word is very similar to knowledge. Communities are the main purveyors of culture, values, and beliefs. They are the centers for education, the arts.

The Intelliville concept is designed to build a center that will attract a combination of high tech startup businesses, research organizations, and education facilities. The location is strategically selected to attract companies that are looking for a remote, safe, gated location where housing is obtainable on site. Similar projects are Baylor University's BRIC (Baylor Research & Innovation Collaborative) and the CTTRP (Central Texas Technology & Research Park), Stanford University's Research Park, Purdue University's Discovery Park, and the "Googleplex" in Mountain View, California. This concept supports the Belton Tomorrow: Economic Development Strategic Plan, attracting young professionals and reducing the brain-drain in the region. (Morgan-Scott, 2014)

Mapping

The mapping of the geographical location is important, especially for investors who are not familiar with the area. This section should provide justification for the project in the particular region and provide statistical information such as social groups, unemployment rates, etc. While mapping, I used information from the Metropolitan Statistical Area (MSA) and the local Chamber of Commerce. Please be sure that your data is up-to-date. Here is an example of what I wrote:

Why Central Texas?

The Killeen-Temple-Fort Hood Metropolitan Statistical Area (MSA) has an estimated population of nearly 380,000 people. Bolstered by the dynamic and growing presence of Fort Hood, the greater Killeen region has experienced tremendous growth that will last well into the future. Fort Hood is the single largest economic engine, of not just Killeen, but the central Texas Region. The Army base has seen significant growth over the years, and that growth has impacted the surrounding cities.

Appelbaum (2012) cited in The New York Times that Texas is the future. The Texas economy grew by 3.3% in 2011. The growth was broad-based, not just in the areas of oil or manufacturing. In 2011, Texas accounted for 8.7% of the nation's economy, up from 7.4% a decade prior to 2011. According to the report Rich States, Poor States, many state governors are looking at Texas, which has led the nation in job growth over the past three years, as the state with sound economic policies that can be modeled to improve economic growth. Texas also has resources, such as gas, oil, and land that can be accessed. (McNichol and Johnson, 2012; Cowen, 2013; Morgan-Scott, 2014)

Other Areas

I also wrote two other sections entitled "Grow With Us" and "Location," which provided more statistics about the area, including the economic growth, job growth, and the level of traffic in the area that would allow the project to be viable.

It is paramount to place timelines on what the Lord has given you. This can be done through a flyer or in a presentation to stake-holders and investors. The timelines that I have used are one year, three years, five years, and ten years; you can develop timelines appropriate for your project. Your timelines can be reviewed and adjusted when necessary. The brochure is like a road map: the destination will not change, but how you get there and the length of time that it takes will be dependent on available resources. I have found all of the tools in this chapter incredibly helpful; good planning is priceless.

Chapter 9
Strategies for Success

Sound strategies will aid the survival of the vision, your personal survival, and the survival of your team members. I have learned over time that when developing a vision, it is imperative to adopt a fourfold strategy that embraces prayer, worship, activism, and declarations:

Prayer

The Church and its leadership must love to pray at all times. The altar must become our resting place; we cannot function on our gifts and callings alone—that is very dangerous. Prayer keeps us connected to our Father and provides a covering from the enemy. Without that covering, the enemy has a legal right to our minds and heart. The process of getting into a backslidden state is subtle, and many times, you can be there and not even realize it. Your love relationship with God has simply weakened or even broken down. As we prepare to enter into prayer, Dr. N. Cindy Trimm (2003) suggests five ways that we should check our spiritual armor:

1. Make certain you are properly adorned (Ephesians 6:13–17).

2. Put on the Lord Jesus Christ, and make no provision for the flesh—lust, envy, strife, bitterness, fornication, hatred, etc. (Romans 13:14, Galatians 5:19–21).

3. Confess sins (Psalm 24:3–5, Proverbs 28:13).

4. Examine yourself and determine if you need to repent of something or release (forgive) someone.

5. Cast your cares and burdens upon the Lord. Remember you do not fight spiritual battles in your own strength; you fight them in the strength of the Lord (Trimm, 2003, 1).

Prayer cultivates the spirit of the watchman; you will be able to see the enemy coming from afar. Prayer will lead you to the Word and give you direction and instruction. (Too many leaders only enter the Word when they are preparing to preach.) Prayer will cause you to set yourself apart as a vessel consecrated unto the Lord, and you will be very careful what you let into your spirit because what goes in will manifest through your character and actions. Guard your heart, your calling, and your anointing with all diligence. "Be sober, be vigilant; because your adversary the devil, as a roaring lion, walketh about, seeking whom he may devour" (1 Peter 5:8).

Prayer is critical to opening the heavens, and this access allows you to…

o   see Jesus,

o   see what is happening or what is about to happen,

o   hear the sound of the trumpet which signifies urgency, and

o   wait on the Lord for the appointed time.

Sometimes you may need to seek godly counsel to ensure that the word you heard in prayer was accurate

Without prayer, we are vulnerable to depression, burnout, health issues, etc. Prayer brings strength and encouragement that allows us not to give up on or abort the vision. Love and blessings to you as you walk this awesome journey in Christ Jesus; it is an honor to be chosen by Him, to not only represents Him in the earth but to also maintain His will in the earth.

Worship

Worship is beautiful because it is not predicated on what God has done for us but on who He is. In worship, we glorify, honor, praise, exalt and please God. Our worship must show our adoration and loyalty to God, for who He is. We must do the following in our time of worship:

- ○ Invoke the presence of God.

- ○ Produce a prophetic sound in worship, offering up pure worship, to hear a prophetic word in response.

- ○ Tune into the sound of heaven to get God's attention, that His train or His glory would fill the temple.

There are times when our church will have a divine visitation from the Lord because we spend time in worship; this kind of worship is not accessed in a few minutes but sometimes the majority of the service. We often quote this Scripture: "It is the glory of God to conceal a thing: but the honour of kings is to search out a matter" (Proverbs 25:2). The Lord showed us that we have to get into the glory realm to access His secrets. The door to the glory realm is pure, unadulterated worship.

Activism: Faith and Works

You must become an especially active, vigorous advocate of the cause that the Lord has given you in order to push forward the kingdom of heaven on earth. At the same time, you must vigorously oppose that which is hindering a move of God in your church or your region. Recognize that all involved, everyone in the house, is on assignment, but you must determine his or her assignments! Uzziah was strategic; he developed companies of soldiers that went out to war with him. Each company had a particular focus or responsibility; he had mighty men of valor who had mighty soldiers that made war with mighty power (read 2 Chronicles 26). Everyone cannot have the same focus; roles and assignments must be determined and clarified for all involved.

Declarations

It is of paramount importance that the church is aware of her mandate, her call, and the power and authority that the Lord Jesus has placed within her. Over the years of studying, preaching, and teaching, the Lord has solidified the following declarations in my heart. I believe there are precepts and principles that will release the mandate of God over our lives, and I would often repeat these declarations:

1. This body of Christ, the ministry, and the vision will not die but engage in the next move of God.

2. The relief or the Comforter has come, and we will hear and respond to the global sound.

3. God is mobilizing His people—Mobilization is the making ready a people or group for movement or active service.

4. We will know our enemy, the spirits that we war with, both personally and in the church.

5. We will identify and work with other organizations or movements of God.

6. We will activate our five senses in the realm of the spirit.

7. We are at a moment of divine convergence in which the tipping bowls of prayers are about to be poured out. Those who have been hidden with the governmental mandate will begin to come to the forefront.

8. We are in the season of "suddenlies" and astonishments.

9. There is a breaking forth and a breaking out; we have favor with God.

10. The church must position herself to hear from the heaven; much prayer, supplication, and dedication is needed.

11. We recognize that the battle is over the seed! National deliverance comes through the birth of a promise! We will not abort the seed, the vision or the dream. The seed is the hope of the nation. God is a generational God! "For I reckon that the sufferings of this present time are not wor-

thy to be compared with the glory which shall be revealed in us. For the earnest expectation of the creature waiteth for the manifestation of the sons of God" (Romans 8:18–19).

12. We are a seat of influence, and we must protect the DNA of God.

13. We have a champion's anointing, mandate, and mantle.

14. We will not be discouraged in this season of transition or metamorphosis—God multiplies through division.

15. We will know the Word, and we will know what we are going to bring to the table.

16. We will control our spirits; God is about to trust us with revelation and secrets.

17. We are the trees of righteousness and the leaves of healing for our nation.

18. We will make the right kingdom alliances that will cause us to accelerate.

19. We declare that the heavens will shake and the earth will move during our legislative intercession.

20. We will move in the anointing and the authority of the "dimensionalist," stepping into eternity and changing the atmosphere before time catches up.

I also held on to the following Scripture:

> But thou, O LORD, shalt endure forever; and thy remembrance unto all generations. Thou shalt arise, and have mercy upon Zion: for the time to favour her, yea, the set time, is come. For thy servants take pleasure in her stones, and favour the dust thereof. So the heathen shall fear the name of the LORD, and all the kings of the earth thy glory. When the LORD shall build up Zion, he shall appear in his glory. He will regard the prayer of the destitute, and not despise

their prayer. This shall be written for the generation
to come: and the people which shall be created shall
praise the LORD. (Psalm 102:12–18)

We are in the season of the "set time" of the church. The stage is
set, the people are positioned (both on and off stage), and the curtain
is about to be drawn; it is time to perform. Like a film set, we somehow can hear, "Lights, camera, action!" The season for the church
to negotiate with the world systems is over, and we are now in the
process of a takeover. Our season is now, and it is a certain and sure
time for the set women and men of God to emerge. Metaphorically
speaking, the people of Zion are a troop or a nation of people that
will lead this nation and indeed the world out of a dry, solitary place
where she has failed to acknowledge the Lord Jesus Christ as King.

I heard the Lord say the following regarding the church, the
remnant:

1. She has been pregnant with expectancy for a while.

2. The baby was breached, and God is repositioning things
    so that the promise can come forth.

3. Now we have to get ready to push because things are going
    to move quickly, at an accelerated rate.

4. It seemed like things were stuck for a while. We could feel
    the movement but not the manifestation, but the season
    has changed.

5. Methodology and strategy, skills, and the application will
    begin to come to you.

Walk Through the DOOR

We must identify and walk through the doors that God has opened for us, but the doors can only be accessed through the following:

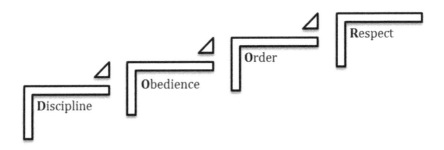

This stage of the process is going to take discipline in our lives; we cannot give up at the first hurdle. Obedience to the word and operating in order are critical for any vision to be effective. Respect for the Lord and others will cultivate integrity of heart, bringing authenticity and credibility to the vision. Everyone filled with the Holy Ghost must have a concept of the heavenly vision and where he or she fits in the eternal plan of God in the earth realm. We must take the time to seek the mind and will of God concerning our ministry, our community, and our nation. We must know where we fit.

There is a king or queen in you. However, you cannot take back what you did not know was stolen from you. Psalm 8:4–6 say, "What is man, that thou art mindful of him? and the son of man, that thou visitest him? For thou hast made him a little lower than the angels, and hast crowned him with glory and honour. Thou madest him to have dominion over the works of thy hands; thou hast put all things under his feet." You must discover and embrace the king or queen in you.

During this season, God will increase our discernment. With discernment comes authority and responsibility. Every vision from heaven comes to establish in the earth realm what is already legislated in the heavens. We declare that we will understand the heavenly vision and our purpose! Understanding the vision of the Lord is essential. Prior to doing so, the Apostle Paul did things that were contrary to God's will, and he was against the followers of Christ.

> But rise, and stand upon thy feet: for I have appeared unto thee for this purpose, to make thee a minister and a witness both of these things which thou hast seen, and of those things in the which I will appear unto thee; Delivering thee from the people, and from the Gentiles, unto whom now I send thee, To open their eyes, and to turn them from darkness to light, and from the power of Satan unto God, that they may receive forgiveness of sins, and inheritance among them which are sanctified by faith that is in me. Whereupon, O king Agrippa, I was not disobedient unto the heavenly vision. (Acts 26:16–19)

Once we understand the vision of the Lord, that vision is going to accelerate us, causing us to develop our craft and advancing us to the level of greater works. We must make ourselves available because the Lord wants to move us quickly into strategic places of influence where we will operate innovatively and creatively. Acceleration is directly proportional to force; it increases or decreases linearly with an increase or decrease in force if mass remains constant. Moral, spiritual, and social crises are forcing us to come out of hiding and take our places quickly. Do not hesitate; know God's will concerning you, and move in it boldly. With this reality in mind, I found it necessary to make further declarations. The words of our mouths can be a powerful source of life, and some of these declarations may help you:

1. We declare and decree that every hidden agenda of the enemy is exposed and torn down.

2. We declare and decree that we will not bow to the agenda of man or the enemy. If God said it, we believe it; that settles it!

3. We declare and decree that every false prophecy is rendered fruitless and the mouth of every naysayer is made dumb.

4. We declare and decree that this house is established upon Jesus Christ the Solid Rock. This ministry belongs to God; He is the head of the church and the ruling authority in this house.

5. We declare and decree that we are shifting in anointing and inheritance from the kingdom of Saul to the kingdom of David.

6. In 1 Corinthians 4:20, it reads, "For the kingdom of God is not in word, but in power." We declare and decree that we shall not move in idle words but in the power of the kingdom.

7. Psalm 145:13 reads, "Thy kingdom is an everlasting kingdom, and thy dominion endureth throughout all generations." We declare and decree that we have tapped into the plan of the everlasting kingdom.

8. Psalm 103:19 reads, "The LORD hath prepared his throne in the heavens; and his kingdom ruleth over all." We declare and decree that we shall rule over all in this region, according to the predestined will and plan of God.

9. We declare and decree, according to Joshua 1:2, we shall possess the land that the Lord has given us.

10. We declare and decree, we shall not be intimidated by the rivers ahead of us (Joshua 3:13).

11. We declare and decree we shall build kingdom relationships that will propel the vision of the house and God's heart concerning us.

12. We declare and decree we will not feel overwhelmed by the task ahead of us.

13. We declare and decree we will not experience defeat.

14. We declare and decree we shall break through all seemingly impenetrable barriers.

15. We declare and decree we shall be a unified force.

16. We declare and decree the ark of the Lord (representing the command of the Lord, the provision of the Lord, and the miracles of the Lord) and the glory of the Lord shall go before us, lead us, and direct us.

17. We declare and decree we shall possess the gates of the region.

18. We declare and decree we shall be an apostolic center.

19. We declare and decree the blessings of heaven and earth shall be released unto us.

20. We declare and decree the promised seed is protected from the plan of the enemy.

Chapter 10

Conclusion

My transparency in my own journey as a visionary was to hopefully encourage someone in his or her journey in becoming a visionary; assisting individuals, churches, and businesses in developing their vision. I have learnt as people, whenever we read a story or hear a report on the news; we often make a judgment based on partial information. Human nature often makes us opinionated and quick to judge without all the facts or without taking a deeper look at the scenario presented to us. I heard a wise man teach that the babes speak first then think later; a mature person will think first and then carefully craft his or her words later. The mature saint realizes that words have life as we maneuver in a voice-activated kingdom. When you have the spirit of your heavenly Father, then you walk in the spirit of creative power, "In the beginning God created…" (Gen. 1:1) and then we go on to read, "And God said…" (Gen. 1:3).

As we face the current economic crisis in this nation and periodic potential government shutdowns, it is very easy to fall into the mode of complaining and speaking the obvious. God has started to challenge me to look a little deeper and to be careful what I speak into the atmosphere. I have been reminded that when I read the scriptures, I need to always ask the spirit of God to help me unlock the text, to give the revelatory meaning of the word of God. It is imperative to do the same with the current economic, political, social and moral crisis and what my response should be. The Lord reminded me that He is the one that has the heart of man in His hands. In the scriptures, we read about the instruction that God gave to Moses as He was preparing him to walk the children of Israel through a deliverance process.

"And the LORD said unto Moses, When thou goest to return into Egypt, see that thou do all those wonders before Pharaoh, which I have put in thine hand: but I will harden his heart, that he shall not let the people go" (Ex 4:21).

I have now begun to ask a different set of questions as this nation is being held hostage to the ideals of humanism, the issues now become deeper than a political issue and the nature of my assignment then changes.

As the church, we are now required to look at the hidden picture: What is going on in the realm of the spirit? What is God trying to show us? What does He want us to do about it? Making the Implicit, Explicit! No matter how we feel initially, we have to remember that God is in control. The church has to take a different approach to ensure that God gets the glory in all things; His wisdom supersedes that of man and God has a plan that we may not yet understand. It is time for us to pray that God be put back on the throne of this nation. The Lord told Moses, "And I will harden Pharaoh's heart, and multiply my signs and my wonders in the land of Egypt" (Ex 7:3). God alone is our source; the believer is now challenged to move in the expectation of the supernatural provision of the Lord Jesus Christ.

The Hebrew word for government is Misrah which means empire, those that prevail over us or those that have power like a prince. The word warns us not to despise government, empire or dominion and not to speak negatively about dignitaries. "But chiefly them that walk after the flesh in the lust of uncleanness, and despise government. Presumptuous are they, selfwilled, they are not afraid to speak evil of dignities" (2 Peter 2:10). I have learned to be responsible for my sphere of influence. We need to pray that fairness and justice in every stratum of society are perpetuated, and how can I move with the heart and mind of Christ and that headship to Christ is returned.

Our global society is continually progressing in ideology, operation, and functionality. It is imperative for leaders to understand that change is an ongoing process, one that we need to be engaged in and be at the forefront of leading. With the many social and moral crises taking place across the world, we are rapidly becoming cognizant of the brokenness that our nations and people groups are facing. Healing for the nations and healing for the people are being sent.

As a nation, we can no longer deny that we have spiritual, social, political, and economic goals to achieve. Healing of communities and nations will require an investment of time, people, and resources. There is so much injustice in our nation and in our communities on so many levels: culturally, politically, socially, and economically. As leaders, we are required to bridge the gaps in our communities. Our discourse and ideology have to change, our respect for life and people has to change, and we need to give more respect and honor to the Word of God. This era of change is an exciting time for vision development. I declare that "eye hath not seen, nor ear heard, neither have entered into the heart of man, the things which God hath prepared for them that love him" (1 Corinthians 2:9). The scriptures encourage us to,

> Enlarge the place of thy tent, and let them stretch forth the curtains of thine habitations: spare not, lengthen thy cords, and strengthen thy stakes; For thou shalt break forth on the right hand and on the left; and thy seed shall inherit the Gentiles, and make the desolate cities to be inhabited. (Isaiah 54:2–3)

God has a plan; He is positioning the nation for the wave of revival that is coming. The latter rain is coming, and the outpouring of the Spirit of the latter rain will bring the crops to maturity and usher in the kingdom of God with a similar but much bigger display of power, one that will be able to shift the courses of our nations. The problems we are facing are systemic, and we need a paradigm shift in the seven mountains. The seven mountains are the strategy used to take dominion in our communities and our nations. The way to take dominion is by taking control of the seven social structures in society called "mountains." They are government, media, family, business and finance, education, faith, and arts and entertainment. As visionaries, motivators, and problem solvers, we must walk in courage, integrity, compassion, humility, and reliability. We must catch the vision and prepare for the transition as we let God arise in our churches, our communities, and our nations. We have to be bold and speak the Word of faith over the vision. The Scriptures declare,

> I will declare the decree: the LORD hath said unto me, Thou art my Son; this day have I begotten thee. Ask of me, and I shall give thee the heathen for thine inheritance, and the uttermost parts of the earth for thy possession. Thou shalt break them with a rod of iron; thou shalt dash them in pieces like a potter's vessel. Be wise now therefore, O ye kings: be instructed, ye judges of the earth. (Psalm 2:7–10)

Let us walk in the Spirit of the Lord, wisdom, understanding, counsel, might, knowledge, and the fear of the Lord (Isaiah 11:2). Let us allow the Lord to use us to lift up a standard of righteousness in our nation (Isaiah 59:19).

The church is on the cusp of her greatest season; let the remnant stand and take her place in all strata's of society. It is time for the real church to stand up and herald her God-given voice to bring back order to this nation. We have to be clearly able to articulate the heart and mind of God concerning His people. If the church does not take her place, not just in Hollywood, but in the political arena also, things are only going to get worse. We have to know how to walk through these open doors with a pure heart, the character and love of Christ, or we will be corrupt and easily bought after we arrive. We cannot sell out the principles of Christ or prostitute our gift…the world must be reintroduced to Jesus Christ as Lord of all, who sacrificed His life at Calvary that a sinful world could be redeemed from the corruptible nature. Jesus said, "…I am come that they might have life, and that they might have it more abundantly" (John 10:10). No matter how far we stray from God, His arms are outstretched waiting for our return.

We now have to reposition ourselves for the divine takeover. Christ is the only one that is constant, sure and never failing. We have to become the lenders, the resource for our community, not just spiritually, but economically. There must be a pooling of resources so that we can be effective, especially as governmental systems slow down, break down or even become corrupted. We should be the ones shaping policy and formulating legislation, the creative thinkers with innovative ideas that will move us through the 21st century and beyond. We have to make time to tap into the eternal, making the invisible visible, moving from prayer to the manifested will of God in the earth realm. There are so many powerful men and women of God who are well able to occupy key roles and positions in society; our season is now. Engage in the kingdom move of God; step into the wave of the release of the supernatural glory and favor of God.

Appendix

Appendix 1

The 21/21 Model

Name of City or Person	Meaning
1. **Oboth**	A mumble or a familiar spirit.
2. **Ijeabarim**	Ruins of the passers.
3. **Moab**	An incestuous son of Lot.
4. **Zared**	To be exuberant in growth; lined with shrubbery.
5. **Arnon**	A brawling stream or to creak (or emit a loud sound).
6. **Amorites**	Publicity—that is, prominence, boast of oneself, declare, or demand.
7. **Ar** (won battles in this place)	A place guarded by waking or a watch.
8. **Beer**	A pit, especially a well.
9. **Mattanah**	A present (a sacrificial offering in a good sense or a bribe in a bad sense).
10. **Nahaliel**	Valley of God, a stream, especially a winter torrent (brook, flood, river, stream, valley).
11. **Bamoth**	Heights: an elevation, height, high place, wave.
12. **Pisgah** (went to the top of this place)	To contemplate or consider.

13. **Jeshimon** (looked toward)	A desolation, desert, solitary, wilderness, to lie waste, be desolate.
14. **King Sihon**	Tempestuous, to wipe away, sweeping.
15. **Jahaz**	To stamp (perhaps threshing-floor).
16. **Jabbok**	Pouring forth, to pour out—that is, to empty, figuratively, to depopulate.
17. **Heshbon** 18. The angels of the Lord had to fight to get through with the message. There has been a great warfare in the heavens.	*Positive*: contrivance (the faculty or power of contriving; a plan or scheme; expedient). By implication, intelligence; device or reason. *Negative*: to fabricate, to plot or contrive (usually in a malicious sense).
19. **Dibon** (place in Heshbon)	To mope, pine, sorrow.
20. **Nophah** (place in Heshbon)	To puff, to inflate, blow hard, give up.
21. **Medeba**	Water of quiet.
22. **Jaazer**	Helpful; to surround—that is, protect or aid.

Appendix 2

Vision Emergence Template (VET)

Sections	Objectives	Project Details
Project Coordinator **Project Consultant**		
Introduction 1. Concept 2. Philosophy 3. Overview		
Mapping Geographical Location		
Job Creation		
Reaching into the Future		
Project Uniqueness		
Qualities of the Leadership Team		

Entrepreneurial Investment		
Stakeholders		
Partners, Helpers, and Donors		
Project Goals 1		
Project Goals 2		
Project Goals 3		
Other Important Components		• Innovative project name • Branding—logo • Every page needs to be bright and colorful • Site map • Photographs • Renderings

Bibliography

Al-Katatsheh, M., and Al-Rawashdeh, M. 2011. "The future of north-south dialogue in the context of globalization." *Journal of Politics and Law*, 4 (2), 108–119. Retrieved from http://search.proquest.com/docview/892569533?accountid=34899.

Barna Group. March 9, 2016. *Americans Struggle to Talk Across Divides.* https://www.barna.com/research/americans-struggle-to-talk-across-divides/.

Bismark, T. 2012. *Dimensions, Atmospheres and Climates.* Audio collection. www.tudorbismark.org.

Bismark, T. 2008. *The Spirit of Honor.* C4Promotions.

Bernatowicz, H. June 15, 2011. *String Theory for Kids, Teens, even Adults.* https://stringtheory4kids.wordpress.com.

Cardoso de Sousa, F., Pellissier, R. and Monteiro, I. (2012). *Creativity, Innovation and Collaborative Organizations.* The International Journal of Organizational Innovation Volume 5, Number 1, Summer 2012.

Dalziel, M., and S. C. Schoonover. 1988. *Changing Ways: A Practical Tool for Implementing Change Within Organizations.* New York, NY: American Management Association.

Denning, P. J., and R. Dunham. 2006. "Innovation as language action." *Communications of the ACM*, 49 (5), 47–52. Retrieved from http://vlsicad.eecs.umich.edu/~imarkov/Innovation.pdf.

Derue, D. S., and B. D. Rosso. 2012. *Toward a theory of rapid creativity in teams.* University of Michigan. Retrieved from http://www.

scottderue.com/wp-content/downloads/pdf/theory-of-rap-id-creativity.pdf.

Galan, J. I., J. C. Monje, and J. A. Zuniga-Vicente. 2009. *Implementation Change in Smaller Firms*. Research Technology Management.

Grace, R. 2005. "Age of innovation, creativity is here," *Plastics News*, 17 (25), 1–6. Retrieved from http://web.ebscohost.com.libproxy. edmc.edu/ehost/detail?sid=21015b0f-7bac-4c70-b8e4-6a73f-242acc1%40sessionmgr15&vid=1&hid=12&bdata=JnNpd-GU9ZWhvc3 QtbGl2ZQ%3d%3d#db=bsh&AN=18130391.

Mangra, M., M. Stanciu, M., and G. Mangra. 2009. "Globalization—A contradictory but offensive process." *Revista Academiei Fortelor Terestre*, 14 (4), 81–87.

Morgan-Scott, C. 2013. "Total Quality Management in High School Education Accountability Measures: An Innovative Approach," *Argosy University*. Phoenix, AZ.

Prosci. 2016. *Change Management Measurement and Metrics*. https://www.prosci.com/change-management/thought-leadership-library/measuring-change-management-effectiveness-with-metrics.

Schoonmaker, J. 2006. "Organizational culture types," *Grand Rapids Business Journal*, 24 (33), B3. Retrieved from MasterFILE Premier database.

Shields, C. 2009. "Transformative leadership: a call for difficult dialogue and courageous action in racialised contexts," *International studies in educational administration* (Commonwealth Council for Educational Administration & Management (CCEAM)), 37 (3), 53–68. Retrieved from Academic Search Complete database.

Trimm, N. C. 2003. *Rules of engagement*. Volume 1. Kingdom Life Publishing Company.

Wagner, C. P. 2002. *Spheres of Authority: Apostles in Today's Church*. Wagner Publications. Colorado Springs, Colorado.

Weiner, E. 2003. "Secretary Paulo Freire and the democratization of power: Toward a theory of transformative leadership,"

Educational Philosophy & Theory, 35 (1), 89. Retrieved from Education Research Complete database.

Zimmerman Jones, A., and D. Robbins. 2016. *The Basic Elements of String Theory.* Dummies. http://www.dummies.com/education/science/physics/the-basic-elements-of-string-theory/.

References

Al-Katatsheh, M., and Al-Rawashdeh, M. 2011. "The future of north-south dialogue in the context of globalization." *Journal of Politics and Law*, 4 (2), 108–119. Retrieved from http://search.proquest.com/docview/892569533?accountid=34899.

Appelbaum, B. June 5, 2012. "Texas Is the Future," *New York Times* [New York]. Retrieved from economix.blogs.nytimes.com/2012/06/05/texas-is-the-future/?_r=0, from New York.

Ashley, R. 2010. "Green Home Building Trends for 2010," *International Business Times*. Retrieved from http://www.ibtimes.com/contents/20100428/green-home-building-trends.htm

Austin, J. 2003. *The Breaker Anointing. Master Potter*. https://www.masterpotter.com/newsletters/article.asp?id=62.

Bismark, T. 2009. *The Order of the Kingdom*. C4Promotions.

Caron, A. *Apostolic Centers: Shifting the Church, Transforming the World*. Arsenal Press. Colorado Springs, Colorado.

Cowen, T. 2013. "Why Texas is Our Future," *Time*, 182 (18), 30.

Cumming, T. G., and C. G. Worley. 2005. *Organization Development and Change* (8th ed., pp. 203–204). Mason, OH: Southwestern College Publications.

Dalziel, M., and S. Schoonover. 1988. "Changing Ways—A Practical Tool For Implementing Change Within Organizations," *AMACON a division American Management Association*. Retrieved from http://www.stevezuieback.com/pdf_leadership/chaningwaysleadership.pdf.

Eckhardt, J. 1999. *Moving in the Apostolic.* Renew Books. Ventura, CA.

Feld, B. 2012. "Startup communities: Building an entrepreneurial ecosystem in your city," *Wiley.* Hoboken, N.Y.

Freed, S. 2007. *Destiny Thieves: Defeat Seducing Spirits and Achieve Your Purpose in God.* Chosen Books. Grand Rapids, MI.

Generals International. 2016. *The Seven Mountains of Societal Influence.* https://www.generals.org/rpn/the-seven-mountains/.

Goll, J. W. 2004. *The Seer: The Prophetic Power of Visions, Dreams, and Open Heavens.* Destiny Image. Shippensburg. PA.

Killeen Chamber of Commerce. 2014. Retrieved from http://www. killeenchamber.com/.

Icelandic Online Dictionary and Readings. November 2016. Lexium. http://digicoll.library.wisc.edu/cgi-bin/IcelOnline/IcelOnline. TEId-idx?type=simple&size=First+100&rgn=lemma&q1=lexi um&submit=Search.

Mangra, M., M. Stanciu, and G. Mangra. 2009. "Globalization—A contradictory but offensive process," *Revista Academiei Fortelor Terestre*, 14 (4), 81–87.

McNichol, E., and N. Johnson. 2012. *The Texas Economic Model: Hard for Other States to Follow and Not All It Seems—Center on Budget and Policy Priorities.* Retrieved from http://www.cbpp. org/cms/?fa=view&id=3739.

Moresco, J. 2009. "4 Green Building Trends to Watch in 2010," *Gigaom.* Retrieved from http://gigaom.com/cleantech/4-green-building-trends-to-watch-in-2010/.

Moskowitz, C. 2012. *5 Reasons We May Live in a Multiverse.* http:// www.space.com/18811-multiple-universes-5-theories.html.

National Association of Home Builders. 2011. Retrieved from http:// www.nahb.org.

Olukoya, D. K. 1999. *Prayer Rain.* Mountain of Fire and Miracle Ministries. Lagos, Nigeria.

Peretti, F. E. 2003. *This present Darkness.* Crossway. Wheaton, Illionis.

Price, P. A. 2006. *The Prophet's Dictionary*. Whitaker House. New Kensington, PA.

Price, P. A. 2008. *The Prophet's Handbook: A Guide to Prophecy and its Operation*. Whitaker House. New Kensington, PA.

The official string theory website. 2016. *Looking for extra Dimensions: What is a dimension.* http://www.superstringtheory.com/experm/ exper5.html

Williams. M. November 7, 2016. *A Universe of Ten Dimensions.* http:// www.universetoday.com/48619/10-dimensions/#ixzz2UyUxSu4B

Wagner, C. P. 1993. *Breaking strongholds in your city: How to use spiritual mapping to make your prayers more strategic, effective, and targeted (The Prayer Warrior Series)*. Regal Books. Ventura, CA.

Wagner, C. P. 1992. *Prayer Shield: How to Intercede for Pastors, Christian Leaders, and Others on the Spiritual Frontlines (The Prayer Warrior Series)*. Regal Books. Ventura, CA.

Wagner, C. P. 1992. *Warfare Prayer: How to Seek God's Pewer and Protection in the Battle to Build His Kingdom (Prayer Warrior)*. Regal Books. Ventura, CA.

The Future

Thank you for taking the time to read this book. I pray that it was a blessing, motivating and equipping you to take your vision to the next level. Please let me know how this book has impacted you; I would love to hear from you.

Part two of my book will be released in September 2019; I will share the unfolding of the vision, providing practical guidelines to assist every visionary.

For consulting services or speaking engagements please feel free to visit my website, www.claudettemorganscott.com. You can follow me on Facebook, Twitter or Instagram.

I am excited to assist in the development of your God-given vision. I look forward to hearing from you!

About the Author

Dr. Claudette Morgan-Scott holds a doctoral degree in business administration and a master's in public sector management. She is the senior pastor and the president of Shiloh Worship Center Inc. in Belton, Texas. She has worked in the field of education and management for over twenty-five years and in ministry for twenty years.

Claudette has been a public speaker for a variety organizations and faith-based events worldwide. She has lectured in colleges and universities all over the world, in the area of social work and management. She is currently a professor at a local university teaching Strategic Management to undergraduate students.

The author is the principal owner of the consultancy firm, Morgan Scott Management Consultants, LLC. Her dynamic leadership abilities and innovative ideas have been proven through her various leadership responsibilities.

Through her worldwide experience, she brings a unique opportunity to all her clients. Claudette is able to assist in vision casting through the lens of the global marketplace.

Claudette is a visionary, advancing the kingdom of God. She has a unique ability to empower others to seek and pursue their God-given destiny and purpose. Claudette is a firm believer that the church must be the voice of influence in the marketplace, occupying all mountains of society: the church, the family, education, arts and entertainment, business and finance, media, and government. She believes that her kingdom mandate is education and government, and works with community leaders in these areas.

In her role as senior pastor and business consultant, Claudette continues to be very active in leadership development. She has a strong prophetic call on her life, speaking life over nations and people groups. Claudette continues to dedicate herself to assist others and aid them to become successful in their purpose in life. She believes that one of her many assignments is to train, support and undergird leaders in both corporate firms and the faith-based world. She sees her ministry as an intercessor, alter-evangelism, teacher, coach, mentor, and counselor, operating in a strong prophetic anointing, with wisdom and insight.

Lightning Source UK Ltd.
Milton Keynes UK
UKHW042206030522
402417UK00010B/45